INSIGHT POCKET GUIDES

Jamaica

APA PUBLICATIONS

Part of the Langenscheidt Publishing Group

L

Jamaica and the Caribbean

250 miles / 400 km

Atlantic Ocean

Caribbean Sea

UNITED STATES OF AMERICA

Sarasota
West Palm Beach
Fort Lauderdale
Miami
Key West

MEXICO

Cancún
Pinar del Río
Havana
Sa'nta Clara
Sancti Spíritus
Camagüey

ISLA DE LA JUVENTUD

CUBA

GRAND BAHAMA ISLAND
GREAT ABACO ISLAND
Nassau
ELEUTHERA ISLAND
ANDROS ISLAND
CAT ISLAND

BAHAMAS

ACKLINS ISLAND
TURKS AND CAICOS ISLANDS (UK)
GREAT INAGUA

Santiago de Cuba
Guantánamo

HAITI
Port-au-Prince

DOMINICAN REPUBLIC
Santiago
Santo Domingo
San Pedro

HISPANIOLA

San Juan
PUERTO RICO (USA)

VIRGIN ISLANDS (UK)
VIRGIN ISLANDS (USA)
ST. CROIX (USA)

ANGUILLA (UK)
SAINT MARTIN (FR./NL.)
SABA (NL.)
ST. CHRISTOPHER AND NEVIS
MONTSERRAT (UK)

LEEWARD ISLANDS

ANTIGUA AND BARBUDA
GUADELOUPE (FR.)

DOMINICA
MARTINIQUE (FR.)
Fort-de-France

ST. LUCIA
ST. VINCENT
BARBADOS
Bridge-town

GRENADA

WINDWARD ISLANDS

ANTILLES
GREATER
LESSER
ANTILLES

JAMAICA
Montego Bay
Spanish Town
Kingston

CAYMAN ISLANDS (UK)

HONDURAS
Tegucigalpa
La Ceiba

SANTANILLA (HOND.)

NICARAGUA
Managua
León
Lago de Nicaragua
Puntarenas
Volcán Irazú 3432 m
Cerro Chirripó 3819 m
San José
COSTA RICA
Puerto Limón

SAN ANDRÉS (COL.)
PROVIDENCIA (COL.)

PANAMA
Colón
Panama
David

COLOMBIA
Barranquilla
Santa Marta
Montería
Ocaña
Pico Cristóbal 5775 m
Valledupar
Maracaibo
Lago de Maracaibo
San Cristóbal

VENEZUELA
Valencia
Caracas
Petare
Barcelona
Maturín
Pico Bolívar 5007 m
San Fernando de Apure
Río Apure
Ciudad Bolívar
Ciudad Guayana
Río Orinoco

ISLA DE TORTUGA
ISLA MARGARITA

ARUBA (NL.)
CURAÇAO (NL.)
BONAIRE (NL.)

TRINIDAD AND TOBAGO
Port of Spain

GUYANA
George-town

Pacific Ocean

Welcome!

Jamaica is the soul of the Caribbean. Although only 146 miles long and 56 miles wide, it is a continent in miniature, with its own mountain range in the east rising to 7,402 ft, just a few miles from the major city of Kingston. Elsewhere there are colonial estates and wild waterfalls, romantic and remote villages and busy beach resorts. In all, this is an ideal destination for an exotic holiday, with its combination of a very distinctive culture and pristine beaches.

 'Although I was born – and lived the better part of my youth – here, I had to travel and reside in several countries before I could fully appreciate the uniqueness of Jamaica and its people,' says **Sonia Gordon**, Insight's correspondent in Jamaica. In this book Sonia has set out to show you the Jamaica that exists outside the tourist brochures and the often unfavourable newspaper headlines.

Sonia is very well equipped for the role of guide. She has previously worked for the Jamaica Tourist Board, both at home and abroad, but is now back on the island pursuing a career as a freelance writer. Her perspective on the island is both that of a visitor and of an informed insider, the ideal combination for an Insight correspondent.

In this book Sonia has concentrated on the areas popular with visitors – Montego Bay, Ocho Rios and Kingston – although her itineraries also reflect the Jamaica that exists behind the beautiful beaches.

C O N T E N T S

Pages 8/9:
Dunn's River Falls

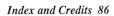

HISTORY &

Although Jamaica is a relatively young country (its documented history begins with the arrival of the Spanish in 1494), historians calculate that it had been occupied from 1000BC to around AD700. But we needn't concern ourselves with that here; we'll skip forward to the end of the 15th century and the arrival of Columbus.

Spanish Rule

When Columbus 'discovered' the island in 1494, he found it populated by a tribe of Arawaks from the Orinoco region of South America. The Arawaks were mostly coastal dwellers, living off the bounty of the sea and a few crops which they planted: cassava, maize, fruit, and tobacco for smoking. They are invariably portrayed as a peaceful people, unaccustomed to hard manual labor. The Spanish were conquistadors, accustomed to having others do their

Columbus meets a native

CULTURE

manual work for them. Within a short period of their arrival, the subsequently enslaved Arawaks had died out, due to overwork, brutality, and European diseases; many committed suicide rather than continue to submit to the harsh life under Spanish rule.

Jamaica became a base for Spanish ships

The most lasting legacy of the Arawaks is the name they gave to the island: they called it **Xaymaca** (meaning land of springs or land of wood and water) from which the name Jamaica derives. Some artifacts of these first Jamaicans have been found in archaeological digs, and can be seen in the village site at White Marl on the way to Spanish Town.

The Spanish brought citrus, bananas, plantain, sugar cane (which dramatically changed the fortunes of the island in later years), cattle, pigs and horses. They also brought the first wave of African slaves to replace the Arawaks, but their relationship with the Africans appears to have been more loosely controlled.

Jamaica's importance to Spain was as a supply base for expeditions to conquer nearby lands; in 150 years of indifferent occupation Spain's most important contribution to the island was to increase the base of the food supply.

The conquistadors built a few settlements – Caguaya (Passage Fort), Savannah-la-Mar, and Puerto Anton (Port Antonio); named a few rivers and left a few other place-names, some of which have been distilled from the original, eg Ocho Rios from Las Chorreras or 'water-falls' probably named after what is now called Dunn's River Falls. Jamaica's first capital under the Spanish was called St Jago de la Vega, today's Spanish Town.

The British and the Pirates

Spain was not the only Old World country seeking new territories to colonize; France and Britain were also hunting competitively. In 1655, having been frustrated in their attempts to conquer nearby Santo Domingo, the British landed on Jamaica's south coast, routed the Spanish, and added Jamaica to their growing list of colonies. Not having found the gold they were seeking, the Spanish rulers had no real use for Jamaica, but a small hard-core of resisters on the island were reluctant to let the British have it. With the

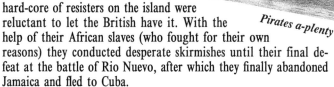

Pirates a-plenty

help of their African slaves (who fought for their own reasons) they conducted desperate skirmishes until their final defeat at the battle of Rio Nuevo, after which they finally abandoned Jamaica and fled to Cuba.

Before they fled, however, they armed and freed the African slaves, who – never having wanted to be here in the first place – were determined not to be enslaved ever again. They could not get back to their homeland, but they could – and did – make life truly miserable for the British in the ensuing years.

I cannot leave the influence of Spain on Jamaica without a word on some of the most colorful inhabitants, the pirates or buccaneers. These men were essentially deserters, escaped criminals, political and religious refugees of various nations, who were bound together by their sworn opposition to the Spanish. They settled in the otherwise uninhabited parts of the Spanish possession of Hispaniola, and their early activities were centered on survival; hunting wild pigs and cattle for meat, hides and tallow which they bartered to passing ships for ammunition and other supplies. The meat was cured on wooden frames called *boucans*, from which the name buccaneer derives.

Their presence in Hispaniola infuriated the Spanish who hunted them relentlessly. In desperation, the buccaneers turned pirates and took to the sea in whatever craft they could lay their hands on. They took their revenge on the Spanish by preying on their ships and killing every Spaniard they could. Each successful capture of Spanish ships swelled their fleet, new recruits joined them and, as they grew bolder, they extended their raids farther.

Port Royal was ideally suited to the buccaneers' needs: it was well situated for harassing the Spanish fleet, there was a ready market for the loot, there were facilities for repairing their vessels, and opportunities for amusing themselves. At first the English officially encouraged them but, shortly after his accession to the throne, Charles II wanted to secure trade with the Spanish colonies and, in 1664, Sir Thomas Modyford was appointed governor of Jamaica with stern instructions to suppress the activities of the buccaneers.

However, the outbreak of the Second Dutch War, in 1665, changed the circumstances again. The Admiralty was unable to spare a fleet for the defense of the island and Modyford was obliged to turn to the buccaneers for assistance. Ruthless, fearless and generally lawless – except among themselves – they proved equal to the task insomuch that a historian of the period was to record: 'It is to the Bucaniers (*sic*) that we owe the possession of Jamaica at this hour.' Modyford's strongest ally among them was a young Welshman, Henry Morgan, who was later to be knighted and made Lieutenant-Governor of Jamaica.

Sugar and Slavery

Sugar was rapidly becoming the new gold of the era, and the Spanish had already introduced sugar cane to the island. The British were quick to realise the potential of this fertile land, but the cane fields were extremely labor-intensive, although profitable for the owners. So thousands of Africans continued to be captured and transported here, to slave in the fields.

Plantations multiplied, and the houses of their mostly absentee owners dotted the island in all directions, and the vast army of slaves needed to run them kept increasing. Historians estimate that the production of sugar brought over 10 million West Africans to the New World in 350 years.

Partly out of fear that they would be outnumbered by the slave population, the British government took the opportunity of solving two problems in one go. Felons and other undesirables from the British Isles were 'encouraged' to relocate in exchange for pardons and offers of land. They were exported here in droves, and gave the names of their home towns to the areas in which they settled all across the island: Aberdeen, Dumbarton, Armagh, Carrickfoyle, Chadworth, Cheltenham, Llandewey, Llandovery etc.

African slaves worked on the sugar plantations

Guerilla Warfare

The birth of a nation is seldom painless and is often achieved by great hardship imposed on the conquered by the conquerors. The settling of early Jamaica was not achieved without difficulty. The Africans did not succumb to slavery without a fight. From the outset of their conquest of the island, the British were harassed by defiant bands of freed slaves who had fled into the mountainous interior and who could not be recaptured. The Spanish word *cimarron*, meaning wild or untamed, was given to this band of freedom fighters; it was eventually corrupted into the word Maroon.

Making peace with the Maroons

From their strongholds in the mountains, the Maroons raided the plantations, set fire to them, made off with livestock and slave women, and generally made life difficult for the British. Their numbers were swelled by runaways from various plantations and eventually, after many skirmishes and all-out wars, the British were forced to sign a treaty granting the Maroons the right to live in peace and freedom, governed by their own laws. In return, they required that the Maroons cease giving shelter to runaways and assist in their recapture.

The two major Maroon villages which remain from those times are Accompong in the Cockpit country in the west, and Moore Town in the mountains of Portland in the eastern end of the island. They are still self-governing – an independent nation within a nation – although, with development and advancing technology, they are less isolated from the rest of the population.

Abolition and After

With the abolition of slavery in 1838, the newly freed peoples fanned out across the country and fresh immigrants swelled the population: 'coolies' as the indentured laborers from India and China were called, were brought in to replace the slaves. Portuguese Jews came, fleeing religious persecution; Palestinians, Syrians, and Lebanese arrive as did Germans who settled their own town, Seaford Town; and trickles of people from other European nations fleeing wars in their homelands and seeking new opportunities. All these added to the Irish, Scots, English, Welsh and the large numbers of Africans, to create a new people called, simply, Jamaicans.

Alexander Bustamante, Jamaica's first Prime Minister, campaigning in the

Out of the struggles of these years emerged some of our National Heroes: Nanny of the Maroons, Paul Bogle, George William Gordon, Marcus Garvey. You can read about them all in more detail in *Insight Guide: Jamaica*.

Jamaica remained a British colony for 307 years; among the more lasting legacies of that period are the British parliamentary system, an independent judiciary, the game of cricket, at which Jamaicans have certainly learned to excel, and numerous plantation houses (called Great Houses) from the era when sugar was as valuable as oil is today. A new constitution, based on universal adult suffrage, was granted by the British in 1944 and Jamaica achieved independence on August 6, 1962.

Jamaica Today

Modern-day Jamaica can be said to have had its beginnings with two cousins of very different personalities and abilities, but whose aspirations were for the betterment of their country.

These two were William Alexander Bustamante, the first prime minister of independent Jamaica, and founder of the Bustamante Industrial Trade Union (BITU) and the Jamaica Labor Party (JLP) who campaigned for some years for true independence; and Norman Washington Manley, founder of the People's National Party (PNP) and the man who secured the constitutional changes that eventually put political power in the hands of the people. Both these outstanding Jamaicans, now deceased, have been elevated to the status of National Heroes.

Under the present system of government, Jamaica is a member of the British Commonwealth with the Queen as titular head of state. Her local representative is the Governor General, whose duties are largely ceremonial. Political power lies with parliament which consists of a house of elected representatives, and a senate whose members are nominated by the prime minister and the leader of the

Rasta men

opposition. General elections are held every five years and the two major political parties, the PNP and the JLP, have formed alternate governments since their inception.

Relative to its size, Jamaica has produced an astonishing number of talented individuals in painting, sculpture, poetry, music, dance, athletics and sports. Jamaicans have formed the nucleus of Olympic track and field teams of Canada and the United Kingdom as well as representing their own country. Indicative of their spirit of fun and competitiveness, they fielded the first bob-sled team from a tropical country in the 1988 Winter Olympics.

Jah! Ras Tafari!

The late Emperor Haile Selassie of Ethiopia, was born Ras Tafari; those who, through interpretation of scriptural passages, acknowledge him as the Messiah, call themselves Rastafarians. But Rasta is not a religion; it is not a cult nor a revolutionary political movement. It is a philosophy for a different approach to life which can be – and has been – adopted by people of different races. The true Rasta, as opposed to the fringe element, is peaceful and hard-working with a tremendous sense of personal dignity.

Their colors are those of the Ethiopian flag – red, green and gold; so popular have these colors become, woven into belts, tams, bags and other craft work, that visitors may be forgiven for thinking that these are the national colors of Jamaica!

Reggae music is identified the world over with Rasta, especially with the superstardom of the late Robert Nesta Marley. But Marley was exceptional and an exception was made for him by the establishment. Rastafarians for the most part have not been accepted by mainstream Jamaica; not in schools nor institutions. Yet some of the most creative people and original thinkers have come out of the Rasta philosophy, which includes some elements the rest of the world disapproves of.

'Legalize It' is the name of a song by Peter Tosh. He was, of course, referring to ganja – or collieweed, marijuana, grass, herb, pot – the plant which Rastas revere in their rituals as 'the weed of wisdom,' in much the same way that the Arawaks used tobacco as a sacred herb.

It is smoked in 'spliffs' (regular cigarette-sized or large paper tubes stuffed with the dried leaves) in chalices (special pipes); it is steeped in white rum or wine and drunk as a tonic; rubbed on insect bites; baked in pastries. Its uses are myriad, as are its users, **and it is illegal**. It is illegal to buy it, sell it, use it, or – worst of all – export it!

Bob Marley statue in Kingston

Historical Highlights

650 Arawaks from the Orinoco settle in Xaymaca.

1494 Christopher Columbus arrives in St Ann's Bay.

1510 First Spanish colonists arrive; establish Sevilla la Nueva – New Seville – on St Ann's Bay. Spanish Town (Villa de la Vega) established on south coast.

1517 First African slaves imported to replace the Arawaks.

1655 British expeditionary force sails into Kingston Harbour, spelling the end of the period of Spanish rule in Jamaica.

1658 Spain makes last desperate bid to hold on to Jamaica in a war which lasted two years – in vain.

1670 Spain cedes Jamaica to the British by the Treaty of Madrid.

1690 Clarendon slaves rebel and escape to join the Maroons, launching the First Maroon War.

1692 Violent earthquake destroys Port Royal, sinking the major part under the sea. Survivors flee across the harbor and settle what eventually becomes Kingston.

1739 Peace treaty concluded between the British and the Maroons, ending the First Maroon War. Peace follows for more than 50 years.

1795 Second Maroon War erupts and drags on for months. Earl of Balcarres imports dogs to track Maroons in the Cockpit country. Balcarres breaks his promise and transports 600 Maroons to Nova Scotia; later moved to Sierra Leone.

1807 Abolition of the slave trade.

1831 Serious slave revolt sparked by Sam Sharpe, a Baptist leader. He was hanged in Montego Bay in the square that bears his name today.

1838 The official end of slavery in Jamaica.

1872 The island's capital transferred from Spanish Town to Kingston.

1907 Violent earthquake destroys most of Kingston, followed by several major fires. The city was subsequently rebuilt.

1938 A series of events, including the Great Depression, create unrest leading to widespread violence and rioting at several sugar estates. Alexander Bustamante emerges as a labor leader, forms the Bustamante Industrial Trade Union (BITU); Norman Manley forms the socialist People's National Party, closely linked with the Trade Union Congress (TUC) and the National Workers' Union (NWU).

1942 Bauxite is discovered on Sir Alfred daCosta's property at Lydford, St Ann. Subsequently, the entire heartland of Jamaica is found to contain bauxite.

1944 Constitution based on universal adult suffrage ends the Crown Colony period in Jamaica's history.

1951 Hurricane Charlie devastates Jamaica.

1962 Jamaica achieves independence from British rule. Bustamante is country's first prime minister. He is succeeded by Donald Sangster who died a few months after taking office; Hugh Shearer succeeds him.

1972 Michael Manley heads a socialist government, forges links with Cuba, and incurs the wrath of the USA. Economy declines and country undergoes period of unrest.

1980 New government led by Edward Seaga takes over with strong economic support from the US. Tourism recovers and expands.

1981 Jamaica and the world mourn death of reggae superstar Robert Nesta (Bob) Marley.

1988 Hurricane Gilbert creates widespread destruction and chaos.

1989 The PNP return to power, first under Michael Manley and then under P.J. Paterson in 1993.

1997 Michael Manley dies.

Jamaica

16 km / 10 miles

Half Moon Bay

Mountain Spring Pt.

Lousy Pt.   **Rose Hall**

Mosquito Cove   **Doctor's**   **Montego Bay**
Lucea   Hopewell   **Cave Beach**   Falmouth   Runa...
        Fort   **Palmyra**   **Greenwood**   **Martha Brae**   **Columbus**
Negro Bay   **Montego**   416 m   **Great House**   (Rafter's Village)   **Rafting**   **Park**
        Governor's   Adelphi   **Good Hope**   Rio Bueno   Discovery Bay
HANOVER   **Coach**   Reading   **Plantation**   Clark's
Green Island   Johns Hall   Town   **Runaway**
        Tryall   **Rocklands**   Wakefield   **Good Hope**   Brown's Town
        Water   **Feeding Station**   Phi...
Bloody   **Dolphin Head ▲ 545 m**   **Wheel**   Montpelier   **Windsor**
Bay   Logwood   **Birchs Hill**   Maroon Town   **Caves**
        Glasgow   **551 m**   **DRY HARBOUR M...**
Negril   Springfield   Ramble   **ST. JAMES**   **TRELAWNY**
        WESTMORELAND   Cambridge   *COCKPIT COUNTRY*   Albert
        George's   *Cabarita R.*   **Orange Hill**   **CORNWALL**   Town   Aboukir
New Hope   Plain   Amity Cross   **641 m**   Quick Step   Wait-A-Bit   Al...
        Little London   Seaford   Accompong   Troy   **Mount Denham**
Broughton   Darliston   Town   **986 m**   Christiana
        Savanna-   Wakefield   Spaldings
        la-Mar   Maggotty   Shooter's Hill   Porus
        Friars Cap. Pt.   **Bluefields**   **Mandeville**
        Newmarket   **Bamboo**
Bluefields Bay   Auchindown   **Avenue**   **ST. ELIZABETH**   Braes River   Patrick Town
        Whitehouse   Middle   R. Black   Gutters   Spur Tree   Toll Gate
                                E. Lacovia   Downs
        Black River   R. Broad   Santa Cruz   **SANTA CRUZ MTS.**   **MANCHESTER**
        Parottee Pt.   **Malvern**   Junction   Spring Plain
Starve Gut   **725 m**   **Malvern**
Bay   Treasure Beach   **Milk River**
        Lover's Leap   Port Kaiser   Alligator Pond   **Bath**
        Cutlass   *Alligator*   Old Womans Pt.   **Milk River**
        Pt.   *Pond Bay*

Caribbean Sea

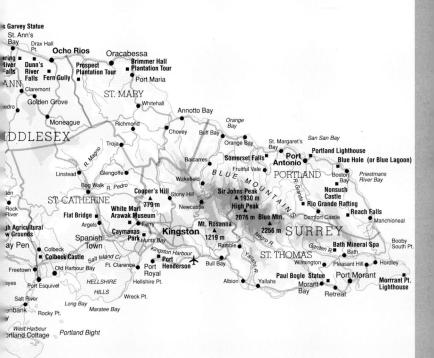

Caribbean Sea

s Garvey Statue
St. Ann's
Bay   Drax Hall
        Pt.   **Ocho Rios**   Oracabessa
ring   Brimmer Hall
iver   Dunn's   Prospect   Plantation Tour
alls   River   Plantation Tour
        Falls   Fern Gully   Port Maria
ANN
        Claremont   ST. MARY
edro   Golden Grove   Whitehall
        Moneague   Annotto Bay   Orange
                        Richmond   Bay
DDLESEX   Troja   Chovey   Buff Bay   St. Margaret's   San San Bay
                                                 Orange Bay   Bay   **Port**   Portland Lighthouse
                            R. Magno   Balcarres   **Somerset Falls**   **Antonio**   Blue Hole (or Blue Lagoon)
        Linstead   Glengoffe   Fruitful Vale   PORTLAND   Boston   Priestmans
                        R. Pedro   Wakefield   B L U E   Bay   River Bay
        Bog Walk   Cooper's Hill   Stony Hill   Nonsuch
ST. CATHERINE   ▲   Sir Johns Peak   Castle
ton   White Marl   779 m   ▲ 1930 m   M   Rio Grande Rafting
Rock   Flat Bridge   Arawak Museum   Newcastle   High Peak   O   Comfort Castle   Reach Falls
River   Argels   2076 m Blue Mtn. U   Manchioneal
h Agricultural   Caymanas   Ferry   Mt. Rosanna   ▲   N
w Grounds Spanish Park   **Kingston**   1219 m   2256 m T   **SURREY**
ay Pen   Town   Hunts Bay   Ramble   A   Garden R   **Bath Mineral Spa**
        Colbeck   Kingston Harbour   I   **St. THOMAS** Bath
        Colbeck Castle Salt Island Cr   Yallahs   N   Wilmington   Pleasant Hill Hordley
Freetown   Old Harbour Bay Ft. Clarence   **Port**   R   S   **Port Morant**
        Port Esquivel   Port   Henderson   Paul Bogle Statue
ayes   Royal   Bull Bay   Albion   Yallahs   Morant   Retreat   **Morrrant Pt.**
        Salt River   Bay   **Lighthouse**
        HELLSHIRE   Hellshire Pt.
enbank   Rocky Pt.   HILLS   Wreck Pt.
y
        West Harbour   Long Bay   Maratee Bay
ortland Cottage   *Portland Bight*

Day itiner

Jamaica is divided into three counties and 14 parishes. Each county has distinctive topography and attributes: Cornwall in the west, central Middlesex, and Surrey in the east. The two main towns and the capital city are each located in separate counties. The mountain range which bisects the island from east to west is largely responsible for the varied terrain, creating slightly different weather patterns in each region.

I have selected Montego Bay and Ocho Rios because they are hubs for the varied attractions offered, they contain the highest concentration of facilities, and are the easiest points from which to arrange day excursions to other places of interest. As the capital and commercial heart of the country, Kingston receives the major share of business travelers, but it is also the repository for the country's historical, theatrical and musical life.

A timeless way to travel

In the western county of Cornwall, my itineraries explore Montego Bay and environs, taking in Negril, parts of the little known south coast and the interior; in central Middlesex, they cover Ocho Rios and environs, with excursions to Port Antonio in the east and a helicopter ride across the country; and in the eastern county of Surrey, I show you the capital city of Kingston and environs, including the Blue Mountains. Wherever you go, mind how you go. On the whole people are friendly, but beware of pickpockets and don't expose yourself unneccessarily to risks.

aRIES

Montego Bay & Environs

1. Highlights of Montego Bay

A relaxing day, seeing something of MoBay and its beaches. Breakfast at Pelican Grill; Montego Bay Highlights tour (Tropical Tours, tel: 952 0400 or 1110); sunbathe and swim at Doctor's Cave Beach; watch the sun set from Marguerite's beer garden.

Montego Bay, in the county of Cornwall, is the most touristy of Jamaica's resorts and, in many ways, is the least Jamaican part of the island. It is unofficially referred to as 'the second city,' Kingston being the capital. To visitors today Montego Bay (popularly 'MoBay') means powder white beaches, clear waters and reggae. To earlier Europeans, the Spanish in particular, it was the port used for shipping lard (fat) from pigs and cattle, and historians believe that the name 'Montego' actually evolved from _manteca_, the Spanish word for lard or butter.

Montego Bay got off to a slow start. A settlement was first established here circa 1655, but people were slow to arrive. Notable events were few and far between. By 1773, Montego Bay had the only newspaper, _The Cornwall Chronicle_, outside of Kingston. Parts of the

Approaching Montego Bay

Doctor's Cave Beach is popular year-round

town were destroyed by fire in 1795 and 1811, and Sam Sharpe, a Baptist preacher and now a national hero, was hung in the square which bears his name, for leading slaves in the area in revolt during the winter of 1831–2. The tourist industry developed around the turn of the 20th century.

Montego Bay's main attraction for a long time was Doctor's Cave Beach, named for Dr McCatty who owned it and turned it into a semi-public bathing club in 1906. It's still a very popular beach with locals and visitors alike, and the hotel strip on Gloucester Avenue has pretty much developed around it.

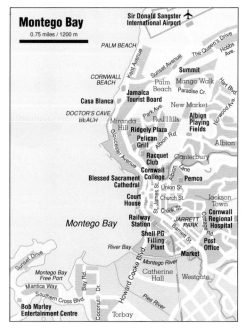

The following day's itinerary works well if you are staying anywhere on the hotel strip. If you are staying at a hotel further out from the town center, it can work very well with a hired car and driver.

The best place for breakfast in Montego Bay is at the **Pelican Grill** (daily 7.30am–11.30pm), east of the hotel strip on Gloucester Avenue. The Pelican has been an institution with locals and visitors alike from as far back as I can remember. The service here is fast and efficient and they do a brisk trade, with freshly roasted and perked coffee, freshly squeezed orange juice, and a choice of American, English or Jamaican-style breakfasts on the menu.

Once you've eaten your fill at the Pelican Grill, then it's time to do some digesting in the sun. You should walk or drive the short distance to **Doctor's Cave Beach** (8am–6pm). There is a small admission fee and the changing rooms, though shabby, are clean. Before 11am, you won't share the beach with a crowd unless it's a holiday or weekend. Then it fills up real fast and by noon it's thick with people. It's the favorite place for Jamaicans to people-watch, sun tan and just hang out, particularly on the raft which is anchored a short distance offshore.

When you are hungry, Gloucester Avenue is thickly populated with cafés and restaurants. If you want to try something local, walk west of Doctor's Cave for about a block to the **Pork Pit** and try some real Jamaican fast food. Chicken, pork or fish is cooked in the special style called jerk and you can have it with hardough bread, festival – a deep fried cornmeal dumpling – or with a slice of roasted breadfruit. An ice cold beer is a good counterpoint to the spicy flavor of the food, and our own lager, Red Stripe, is among the best in the world. It is quite strong, though, so beware *Hits on wheels* of combining it with a hot sun. You may find you are not able to do much more than sit in the shade afterwards.

After lunch, you may want to explore a little. Montego Bay is a confusing city to a non-local driver because of the maze of narrow one-way streets with little or no indication as to the direction of the traffic flow.

An organized tour of the city can help orient you and is less nerve-wracking and risky than trying to figure out the street system yourself. Several tour companies offer city tours but one which I would recommend is the **Montego Highlights** offered by Tropical Tours Ltd. It's a 2½–3 hour drive around the town's historic, residential, commercial and luxury vacation areas, with a special stop at the craft market for shopping if you wish. Tropical Tours is a reliable operator, the drivers are generally courteous and well-informed, and they will collect and return you to your hotel.

Round off your day at **Margueritaville** on Gloucester Avenue, watching the sun dip into a blood red sea as you sit in the beer garden. A lot of people come here to do just that. You can have dinner here too, either in the beer garden, which is casual, or more formally on the seaside patio. You should plan in advance if you prefer the latter choice because reservations are required for dinner (tel: 952 4777 or 3290).

Inside Greenwood Great House

2. Along the Coast

A tour of Greenwood Great House with a 180° view of the horizon; then visit the crocodiles at Jamaica Safari; lunch at Fisherman's Inn and buy a work of art on fabric at Caribatik next door; people-watch from sidewalk cafés on Gloucester Avenue

Although there are several Great Houses in this parish, the two best-known are at Rose Hall and Greenwood. Rose Hall is the more publicized of the two because of the legendary White Witch, Annie Palmer, who is said to have murdered her husbands, ill-treated her slaves, and was finally murdered by them. It's more legend than fact but it draws the crowds. Greenwood has fewer tourist trappings and a more authentic history. It also has the largest collection of rare musical instruments in the Western hemisphere.

Take the A1 past the airport and head east out of Montego Bay for Greenwood Great House, about a 30-minute drive. Hotels you'll pass along the way include two in the Sandals chain of all-inclusive hotels – Montego Bay and Royal Caribbean. Further east is the **Half-Moon Golf, Tennis and Beach Club**, one of the island's top three hotels (the others are Tryall and Round Hill, both in Montego Bay). On a ridge east of the Half-Moon is the **Rose Hall Great House**, built circa 1770 and expensively restored in recent times by a former governor of Delaware in the United States.

Members of the Moulton Barrett family, ancestors of the poet Elizabeth Barrett Browning, are buried in a family plot near Rose Hall, and they lived in the Cinnamon Hill Great House further up the road. Cinnamon Hill was purchased and restored by country-and-western singer, Johnny Cash, a regular visitor to Jamaica and a patron of the Montego Bay

Rose Hall

SOS Children's Village, helping destitute and abandoned children.

Further east past flat, mainly dry marshlands, is **Greenwood Great House** (9am–5pm daily), built by the Barrett family in the latter part of the 18th century. Turn left off the main road at the sign for the Great House and follow the road for about 1½ miles uphill. The present owner-operators Bob and Ann Betton live here, giving this Great House less of a museum feel. The Barretts' library of rare books and old maps is here, as is a wonderful inlaid rosewood piano, a gift from Edward VII to his fiancée, a bathtub made from a solid piece of cedar and much, much more. Many of the very rare musical instruments are in working order and will be demonstrated by the tour guide. From the upper verandah you can actually see the curve of the earth in a 180° arc.

Back on the main road, continue east through the fishing village of Salt Marsh to the **Jamaica Swamp Safari and Crocodile Farm**. This is an interesting tour for the whole family. American Ross Kananga developed this nature reserve and crocodile breeding farm on Salt Marsh Bay, 30 minutes' drive from Montego Bay. A guided tour leads between high wire fences, past the enclosures

Crocodile Farm show

where crocodiles of all sizes bask. The red mangrove swamp (350 acres) can be toured by boat or raft when the water is sufficiently high. There is a bird sanctuary, a petting zoo for children, snakes (in cages) and mongooses – small ferret-like animals which were introduced to Jamaica to rid it of snakes. There are no poisonous

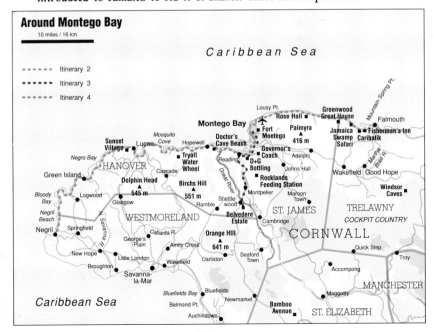

Around Montego Bay

10 miles / 16 km

Caribbean Sea

- ⋯⋯ Itinerary 2
- ▪▪▪▪ Itinerary 3
- ⋯⋯ Itinerary 4

Lousy Pt.

Mountain Spring Pt.

Greenwood
Great House
Falmouth

Rose Hall

Montego Bay
Fort
Montego
Palmyra
416 m

Jamaica
Swamp
Safari
Fisherman's Inn
Caribatik

Doctor's
Cave Beach

Mosquito
Cove
Hopewell
Governor's
Coach
Adelphi

Sunset
Village
Lucea
Reading
D+G
Bottling

Negro Bay
Tryall
Water
Wheel
Cascade
Johns Hall
Wakefield
Good Hope

HANOVER

Green Island

Dolphin Head
545 m

Birchs Hill
551 m

Rocklands
Feeding Station

Montpelier
Maroon
Town

Windsor
Caves

Bloody
Bay
Logwood
Glasgow
Shettle-
wood
Ramble

Negril
Beach

WESTMORELAND

Belvedere
Estate
Cambridge

ST. JAMES

TRELAWNY
COCKPIT COUNTRY

Negril
Springfield
Cabarita R.
Orange Hill
641 m

CORNWALL

George's
Plain
Amity Cross
Quick Step
Troy

New Hope
Little London
Wakefield
Darliston
Seaford
Town

Broughton
Savanna-
la-Mar
Accompong

MANCHESTER

Bluefields Bay
Bluefields
Newmarket
Maggotty

Caribbean Sea
Belmond Pt.
Bamboo
Avenue
ST. ELIZABETH
Auchindown

snakes on the island and the ones exhibited here are large but harmless. Part of the James Bond movie *Live and Let Die* was shot on location here and you can see a five-minute clip of Bond making his escape across the backs of live crocodiles.

The next sizable town is **Falmouth**. Notwithstanding the shabby appearance of the buildings fronting the main road, it remains the best laid out town in the island and several examples of fine Georgian architecture are still standing, particularly on Market Street west of Water Square.

Colorful batik

Just east of Falmouth is **Caribatik** (Tuesday to Saturday, 9am–4pm). The sign is painted in letters 10 ft high so you can't miss it, but drive a few yards further for lunch if you are hungry and return later. (Two interesting restaurants are one door away from Caribatik: the small (12 rooms) but attractive **Fisherman's Inn** whose specialty is catering for divers and deep-sea fishers. You'll probably notice the dive flag flying over the entrance. You can charter boats for big game fishing, dive the reefs along the coast, or simply enjoy a meal at the poolside or indoors. They will also take you across the lagoon to picnic and swim at the beach around the headland. Next to Fisherman's Inn is **Glistening Waters**, a rustic open-air restaurant serving good meals at reasonable prices, which is very popular with hunters in the bird shooting season.

Caribatik is where the late Muriel Chandler established her workshop to create intricate designs on fabric, using the ancient Asian art of batik, a complex method using hot wax and dyes. Her widower, Keith, has maintained the studio, shop and gallery, and the craft is now carried on by young artists. From January through March, you can watch the process of creating designs bythe batik method. Many of the pieces make beautiful wall hangings, unusual and truly Jamaican souvenirs. The shop also sells lengths of fabric and garments for men and women. Take some time to browse in the gallery too, where a lot of Muriel's work is displayed, including a self-portrait in batik.

Caribatik and the restaurants sit on the edge of a phosphorescent lagoon; on moonless nights, microscopic luminous organisms create a firework display underwater when disturbed by fish, a boat, your hand – in fact anything moving through the water.

Back in MoBay, you'll find the town stays up late and the little sidewalk cafés on **Gloucester Avenue** are a good place from which to watch the passing parade. If you like pizza – really great pizza – then **Tony's Pizza** (Gloucester Avenue opposite Cornwall Beach) is the place to be. Visitors and locals hang out at sidewalk tables next to this red and white striped mobile pizza-stand-cum-bar. It opens at night only and stays open until 2am weeknights; and 3am on Friday and Saturday.

3. Estate Tour

Step back in time on Belvedere Estate; dine sumptuously in the cellars of an 18th-century town house, or on the crest of a hill overlooking MoBay, or beside the ruins of a sugar mill on a scenic golf course. As always, take your camera and plenty of film; your swimsuit, suncream and towels too.

You can drive to **Belvedere Estate** (daily 10am–4pm, except Sunday, tel: 956 4710), 30 minutes from downtown Montego Bay, or you can be picked up for a small fee. Either way, this is probably the best estate tour you will experience on the north coast. Follow the map (*see p.25*) past the **Desnoes & Geddes** bottling plant and turn off the main road at Reading. Belvedere is signposted.

Belvedere Estate was one of the first estates to be burnt in the 1831 Christmas Rebellion. It's a working estate of 1,000 acres, which has been designed to recreate plantation life as it used to be in the mid 19th century.

The guided tour begins with a sampling of fruit grown on the property, followed by a drive through the agricultural part of the estate. Then a walking tour along the banks of the Great River, past a working water-wheel and the ruins of the sugar factory in the botanical garden laid out along the banks of the Great and the Bragging Tom rivers. The ruins of the overseer's house stand at the junction of the two rivers.

Traditional dress at Belvedere Estate

A workers' village, replicating the post-emancipation period, contains a herbal garden, a bakery, a blacksmith's, a weaver's home, a potter, a canoe builder and much more. The juice of the sugar cane is extracted by a mule-turned mill and you get to sample the fresh juice after you've watched the process. In fact, you can eat your way around the mini-village, sampling goods at the bakery and the buttery and cook shop.

The tour ends in the **Trash House**, a thatch-roofed building, which duplicates the house where the cane trash was stored, and where you'll finish up with a great, typically Jamaican lunch while a mento band plays for your entertainment. Altogether, a tour not to be missed. Make a day of it, stay and swim if you like.

Dining out in style is one of the pleasures of being in Montego Bay. The following restaurants are in the expensive-but-worth-it bracket, if you want a change of pace and setting. **Norma at The Wharf House** (Reading on the outskirts of Montego Bay. Reservations for dinner, tel: 979 2745). Proprietor Norma Shirley is not only the last word in elegant dining among Jamaicans, her reputation has preceded her overseas: she was one of five internationally recognized chefs invited to appear on the US television program *Lifestyles of The Rich & Famous*, to prepare a meal representative of her country. She was also the only woman in the group. The Wharf House was opened after the success of her Kingston restaurant.

The Town House (16 Church Street, downtown Montego Bay; reservations suggested, tel: 952 2660) is a great favorite with the 'international set' for its sumptuous continental and Jamaican-influenced

menu. Originally housed in the cellars of a Georgian building (circa 1765), The Town House has become something of a Montego Bay tradition. In 1984, the proprietor Jim Snead expanded the restaurant to the first floor which now houses the elegant Blue Room.

Richmond Hill Inn (top of Union Street; reservations suggested, tel: 952 5432, 6107 or 3859) is an old plantation house with a spectacular view of Montego Bay. Dinner is

Sunset over Montego Bay

served under the stars, on a large terrace around a pool and fountain. The menu is strictly continental and the specialty is broiled lobster (in season).

Sitting next to an old, but still active, water-wheel on a golf course is **The Sugar Mill Restaurant** (opposite the Half Moon Hotel; reservations recommended, tel: 953 2314 or 2228). The chef, one of the prestigious *Chaine des Rotisseurs*, has designed an innovative menu around the produce of the island.

4. Day Trip to Negril

Negril has 7 miles of beach on which to swim, suntan, eat and relax. Casual dress, swimsuits, sunscreen and camera a must. It would be unthinkable to be so near Negril – 1½ hours' drive – and not visit this most talked-about resort. The drive there is half the pleasure, so plan to do it leisurely and spend the day.

Follow the A1 west from Montego Bay, past Reading. In the 16 miles between here and the Tryall Golf & Country Club are many large elegant homes, or the entrances to them, many owned by wealthy winter visitors. Shortly after crossing the parish boundary from St James into Hanover, you pass the most exclusive (and expensive) hotel colony in Jamaica, the **Round Hill Hotel**. Its visitors' list reads like a *Who's Who* of international names. Four miles further on, the water wheel of Tryall and the ruins around it can be glimpsed from the road. It is tucked away in dense foliage, but you can park on the grass verge and walk on to the property for a better view and to take pictures. Across the road is

Historic Lucea

the most picturesque (in my opinion) of the championship golf courses to be found on the island. The Johnnie Walker Championship Golf tournament is held here in December each year, and televized for broadcast on the network and sports channels in the United States and elsewhere.

A series of small villages follows, dotted along the coast, before you get to the next town of note, **Lucea**, about 25 miles from Montego Bay. This is the administrative center of Hanover, with some interesting historic buildings. The town center, Sir Alexander Bustamante Square, was dedicated by Queen Elizabeth II during her visit to Jamaica in 1966. Negotiate your way through Lucea with care as there are a few odd turns to make; just watch out for the signs that lead you through to **Green Island**, the next town, and Negril.

Just outside of Lucea is **Rudy Perry's Sunset Village**, offering 'food, drinks, rooms, video and clean washrooms.' The washrooms are basic but are, in fact, clean, and Rudy Perry is a friendly, interesting host who is writing the story of his life and times in the United States. A sign on your right by Cousins Cove points to Blenheim which was the birthplace of Sir Alexander Bustamante.

Stop me and buy one

Seven miles of sand at Negril

Green Island is the last significant village before you enter the long stretch to Negril, and several junctions radiate from the main road here toward Savanna-la-Mar on the south coast.

Negril Cabins is the first resort, on the left, as you enter the area. Beyond the Negril aerodrome is the hotel strip on either side of the road and there is a Jamaica Visitors Information booth next to Cosmo's. It's a good idea to check with them about recommended places to eat, shop, or to find out about the various activities available.

Geraldine Robins, an artist who settled in Negril in 1970, sums up what most people who visit or stay feel about the place: 'Negril is a place that makes everybody, whether they stay at the Grand Lido or in a tent, know themselves…'

Everyone who is just passing through Negril stops at **Cosmo's** at some stage of the journey. It's right on the beach — and once on the beach, you can walk for miles in either direction — the food is excellent, and there is usually an interesting mix of people dropping in for a drink, a chat, a meal, or just to hang out.

Negril is a good place to take children. There's plenty of space, 7 miles of white sand for building castles and running around, and the sea is clear, calm and shallow.

Horseback riding is available at several spots on the beach but check around a bit before you mount. Some of the horses are either straight off the race track or can only be prodded into a desultory trot with effort. Parasailing, scuba diving, water skiing, or simply floating on the surface with a snorkel are some of the ways in which you can spend a totally relaxed day. You can keep the various vendors of shells and carvings, etc. at bay with a simple but firm 'No, thank you.'

Parasailer's view

If you stay until the sun is setting, head for **Rick's Cafe** on the West End. Almost everyone does and for about an hour before sunset the place is alive with a mix of people. Once the sun has disappeared, however, it is deserted within minutes.

Head back to Montego Bay at a leisurely pace for a meal or a nightcap at any of the numerous restaurants or bars listed in the *Eating Out* section at the back of this book. It's a good way to end a relaxing day.

Recreation at Rick's Cafe

30

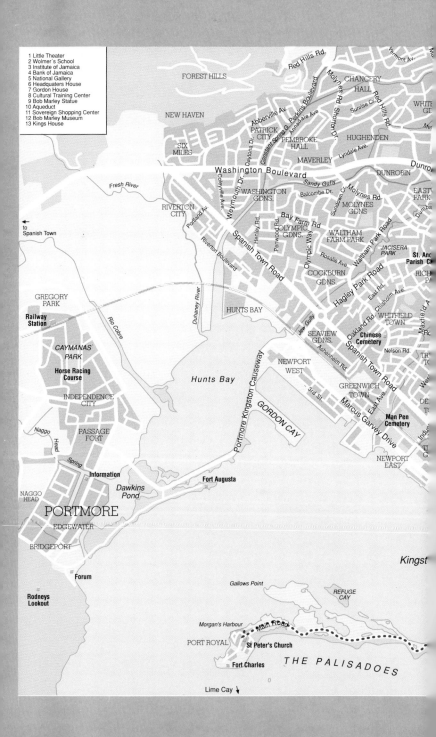

1 Little Theater
2 Wolmer's School
3 Institute of Jamaica
4 Bank of Jamaica
5 National Gallery
6 Headquaters House
7 Gordon House
8 Cultural Training Center
9 Bob Marley Statue
10 Aqueduct
11 Sovereign Shopping Center
12 Bob Marley Museum
13 Kings House

FOREST HILLS

Red Hills Rd.

Vermont Av.

CHANCERY
HALL

WHIT
GI

NEW HAVEN

Abbeville Av.

Molynes Rd. Shorton Dr.

Sunrise Cre.

Red Hills Rd.

PATRICK
CITY

G. Perkins Boulevard

HUGHENDEN

Annadale Ave.

PEMBROKE
HALL

Lyndale Ave.

SIX
MILES

Daytona Dr.

Constant Spring

DUNROBIN

Dunro

Coleyville Ave.

MAVERLEY

Washington Boulevard

Sandy Gully

Fresh River

Weymouth Dr.

WASHINGTON
GDNS.

Balcombe Dr.

C. Molynes Rd.

EAST
PARK

RIVERTON
CITY

Portland Av.

Henley Rd.

Bay Farm Rd

Suddown C.

MOLYNES
GDNS.

Dunba

to
Spanish Town

OLYMPIC
GDNS.

Penwood Rd.

Olympic Way

WALTHAM
FARM PARK

JACISERA
PARK

St. And
Parish C

Riverton Boulevard

Spanish Town Road

Rosalie Ave.

Waltham Park Road

Hagley Park Road

RICH
PA

GREGORY
PARK

Duhaney River

COCKBURN
GDNS.

East Rd.

Chisholm Ave.

Maxfield A

Railway
Station

Rio Cobre

HUNTS BAY

Jew Gully

Oakland Rd

WHITFIELD
TOWN

Rd

CAYMANAS
PARK

Chinese
Cemetery

Nelson Rd.

Ashenheim Rd.

Spanish Town Road

TR
TO

Horse Racing
Course

Hunts Bay

SEAVIEW
GDNS.

NEWPORT
WEST

Wes

INDEPENDENCE
CITY

GREENWICH
TOWN

3rd St.

DE
TO

Naggo
Head

PASSAGE
FORT

Last Ave.

Marcus Garvey Drive

Man Pen
Cemetery

Indu

Spring

Portmore Kingston Causeway

GORDON CAY

TU
G.

Information

NAGGO
HEAD

Dawkins
Pond

NEWPORT
EAST

PORTMORE

EDGEWATER

Fort Augusta

Kingst

BRIDGEPORT

Forum

Gallows Point

REFUGE
CAY

Rodneys
Lookout

Morgan's Harbour

Main Road

PORT ROYAL

St Peter's Church

THE PALISADOES

Fort Charles

Lime Cay ↓

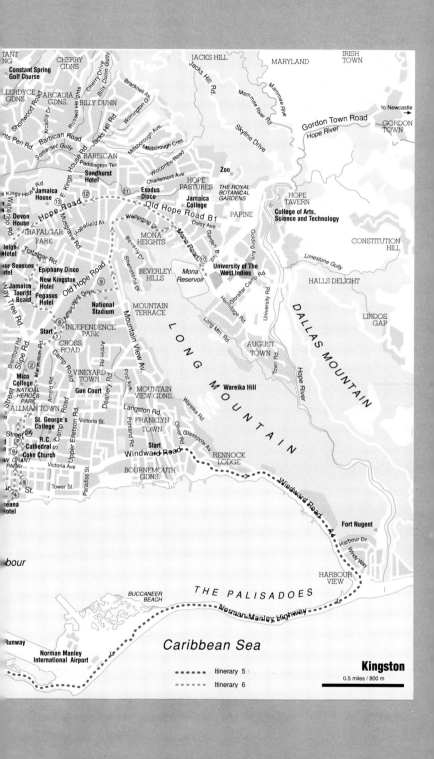

Kingston

0.5 miles / 800 m

•••••• Itinerary 5
•••••• Itinerary 6

Caribbean Sea

THE PALISADOES

Norman-Manley Highway

BUCCANEER BEACH

Norman Manley International Airport

Runway

bour

IRISH TOWN

MARYLAND

JACKS HILL

Jacks Hill Rd.

Mammee River Rd.

Mammee Rive

Skyline Drive

Gordon Town Road

Hope River

to Newcastle →

GORDON TOWN

CONSTITUTION HILL

Limestone Gully

HALLS DELIGHT

LINDOS GAP

DALLAS MOUNTAIN

Hope River

Town Rd.

AUGUST TOWN

Wareika Hill

L O N G   M O U N T A I N

Wareika Rd.

University Rd.

Gibraltar Camp Rd.

Hermitage Rd.

Long Mtn. Rd.

Golding Ave.

HOPE TAVERN

College of Arts, Science and Technology

PAPINE

THE ROYAL BOTANICAL GARDENS

University of The West Indies

Mona Reservoir

HOPE PASTURES

Zoo

Jamaica College

Garden Bd.

Daisy Ave.

Wellington Dr.

MONA HEIGHTS

Mona Road

BEVERLEY HILLS

Beverly Dr.

Shenstone Dr.

Old Hope Road B1

Exodus Disco

Charlemont Ave.

Widcombe Road

Millsborough Cres.

Millsborough Ave.

CHERRY GDNS

Cherry Drive

Billy Dunn Gully

Bracknell Av.

Wilmington Gr.

ARCADIA GDNS.

BILLY DUNN

Barbican Road

Paddington Ter.

BARBICAN

Sandhurst Hotel

Jamaica House

Hope Road

Musgrave Rd.

Hopefield Av.

Arthur Wint Drive.

Old Hope Road

CONSTANT NG

Constant Spring Golf Course

LLERDYCE GDNS.

Shortwood Road

Arcadia Dr.

Somerset Gully

Russell Hts.

Kings House Rd.

Jacks Hill Rd.

nts Pen Rd.

Kings House Rd.

Water Rd.

Devon House

d

TRAFALGAR PARK

Trafalgar Rd.

leigh Hotel

ur Seasons otel

Jamaica Tourist Board

Epiphany Disco

New Kingston Hotel

Pegasus Hotel

ee Rd.

National Stadium

INDEPENDENCE PARK

Start

Slipe Rd.

Brentford Rd.

CROSS ROAD

Camp Road

VINEYARD TOWN

Antrim Rd.

Mountain View Av.

First Ave.

Deanery Rd.

Gun Court

MOUNTAIN TERRACE

MOUNTAIN VIEW GDNS.

Langston Rd.

FRANKLYN TOWN

Portland Rd.

Olivier Rd.

Glasspole Ave.

Start Windward Road

RENNOCK LODGE

Windward Road A4

Fort Nugent

Harbour Dr.

Windy Way

HARBOUR VIEW

Mico College

NATIONAL HEROES PARK

Amold Rd.

Camp Rd.

Upper Elletson Rd.

ALLMAN TOWN

St. George's College

R.C. Cathedral

Coke Church

Victoria St.

Victoria Ave.

Tower St.

Paradise St.

BOURNEMOUTH GDNS.

Street

W. GRANT PARK

St.

eana otel

Kingston & the Blue Mountains

Kingston is the commercial and cultural heart of Jamaica where more than half a million of the island's total population of 2½ million live, making it the largest English-speaking city south of Miami. Most visitors come to Kingston on business, but there is no need to rush off the minute you are through. A tour of the city, for example, will disabuse you of the notion that the entire island is a tourist resort where everyone dances to reggae, says 'yeh mon!,' and aspires to be a DJ artist.

Kingston began as a small, town on the edge of the harbor 300 years ago, but its growth defeated all efforts to order it. Its age is most noticeable in the downtown core, where the urban blight of ghetto dwellings, is a result of the pilgrimage of thousands from the country-side, seeking jobs, fame and fortune, or simply escaping the harsh life of a small farmer.

Kingston, home to 2½ million people

Conversely, much of the island's wealth is controlled by companies and corporations sited here, and is reflected in the sometimes gracious, often ostentatious suburban homes of wealthy or aspiring-to-be wealthy Jamaicans. On some streets, decrepit age and sleek modernity exist cheek-by-jowl. Yet the overall atmosphere is one of irrepressible vigor and youthfulness, reflected most strongly in the people who live here.

It is a bustling, noisy, vibrant city, its vibrancy expressed particularly in the diversity of its artistic and cultural life and the entrepreneurial pursuits of its citizens.

With the closure of the Oceana Hotel downtown, you'll probably be staying at one of the several hotels in the city center, otherwise known as uptown. The heart of uptown is New Kingston's commercial and residential sector and, from here, it is easy to find your way about. Being a business city, most of the fun and recreation takes place after working hours or on weekends. But there are still things that a visitor can do and places to see during the day.

34

5. Kingston

A tour of the city's points of interest: Institute of Jamaica and the Natural History Museum, the National Gallery, the Mona campus of the University of the West Indies, Bob Marley Museum and Devon House. Finish with tea at the Ivor Guest House.

To get to the institute, find your way to Knutsford Boulevard and follow the route on the map (*page 32–33*), a vital reference as many streets have lost their name posts. Most Kingstonians drive by built-in radar and are hard-pressed to recall long lost street names.

Your drive downtown will take you past the **Little Theatre** on Tom Redcam Drive, built in 1961 by Henry and Greta Fowler, founders of the Little Theatre Movement in 1942. The theater is used throughout the year, with two annual seasons here: the internationally-known National Dance Company (NDTC) and the Jamaica Folk Singers. Next to The Little is a public library.

Heroes Park

On your right as you approach the round-about is the headquarters of the Anglican Diocese; on the left is **Up Park Camp** – or just 'Camp', established in 1784 for the British regiments which were stationed here. It is now the headquarters of the Jamaica Defence Force (JDF).

The next street you will reach is Marescaux Road. It has several places of historical interest and two notable schools. The first on your right as you proceed is **Mico College**, one of the oldest teacher-training institutions in the world. Immediately next door is **Wolmer's School** founded over 300 years ago as a boys' school. The girls' school is of later origin.

Opposite Wolmer's School is a large, dusty common, formerly known as Kingston Race Track, the site of horse racing in colonial days. After independence in 1962, a shrine with monuments to the island's national heroes was established at the southern end and it was re-christened **National Heroes Park**. Also at this end of the park, on the traffic island facing it, is a monument to revolutionary Simon Bolivar. Known as 'The Liberator' for his struggles to free Latin American colonies from Spanish rule, Bolivar lived briefly in Jamaica in 1817, and the monument was a gift from Venezuela.

Mico College

The road curves round the park to East Street. On your left, where it intersects with North Street, is the Gleaner Building, home to Jamaica's oldest newspaper, *The Daily Gleaner*, founded in 1834.

The main buildings of the **Institute of Jamaica** (Monday to Thursday 9.30am–4.30pm, Friday 9.30am–3.30pm) are on the corner of East and Tower Streets. Founded in 1879 for the encouragement of literature, science and art, its divisions include the National Gallery, the Cultural Training Center (incorporating schools of art, dance, drama and music), a Junior Center (opposite the East Street headquarters) and an African Caribbean Institute (researching African traditions in Jamaica and the Caribbean) as well as a Publications Division.

The East Street building contains the two major collections of the institute: the **Natural History Division** (entrance on Tower Street) which includes a small, well-laid-out museum, a herbarium, exhibition halls and lecture rooms. The **National Library of Jamaica** (entrance on East Street and formerly the West Indian Reference Library) contains the largest collection of West Indian material in the world. You are not allowed to take bags or hand luggage into the library so it's best to lock it in the trunk of your car.

At the bottom of East Street your route swings past Nethersole Place, location of the Bank of Jamaica, the island's central bank and clearing house, before you turn left then right on Ocean Boulevard. The **National Gallery** is in the Roy West Building (Orange Street, Monday to Friday 11am–4.30pm) behind Kingston Mall and the entrance fee is around US$1. It has the largest permanent collection of works by some of Jamaica's most talented artists, and a busy schedule of temporary exhibitions including the Annual National Exhibition, a tradition since the 1940s, from about the end of November for three to four months.

Your return route takes you north up Duke Street, once a prestigious address for law firms, several of which are still here. Further along Duke Street is the building in which parliament used to meet, the 18th-century **Headquarters' House**. It now meets in **Gordon House** opposite, which was named in honor of George William Gordon, legislator and National Hero, who was executed on suspicion of inciting the 1865 Morant Bay Rebellion.

The last two buildings of note as you leave Duke Street are the island's only Jewish Synagogue, and the octagonal St Andrew Scots Kirk (built circa 1814), Jamaica's first Presbyterian church, which are both on your right.

Make a detour to the right off Tom Redcam Drive at the Little. This will bring you past the **Cul-**

Pomp at Headquarters' House

Budding students

tural **Training Center** on your left (one of the divisions of the Institute of Jamaica). The center trains teachers for the island's schools as well as instructing students, and accepts a limited number of students from overseas. The center contains the schools of art, drama, dance and music.

At the far end of Arthur Wint Drive is the **National Arena**, the venue for a variety of indoor sports and activities. Most recently, it was the setting for His Holiness, Pope John Paul's televized message to Jamaica, before an invited audience, during his visit.

The **National Stadium** next to the Arena was built as part of the independence celebrations in 1962. It is used for major sporting events and concerts requiring a large seating capacity, notably on the occasion of Nelson Mandela's visit. At the entrance to the stadium is a statue of an athlete by sculptor Alvin Marriott. Opposite the stadium, on Arthur Wint Drive, is a statue of the Hon. Robert Nesta Marley, known to his fans simply as Bob Marley.

Turn left at the end of the road on to Mountain View Avenue and drive on to the traffic lights at the junction with Old Hope Road. Turn right on Old Hope Road and follow the map (*page 32–33*) to Mona Road. About five minutes' driving should bring you to the Mona dam (right) and under one of the remaining 18th-century stone aqueducts.

The university's chapel

The **University of the West Indies** (UWI) is built on a square mile of the former Hope Sugar Estate and water was carried by these aqueducts to the sugar mills. The main entrance is a short distance up on your left. UWI was founded in 1948 and opened with 32 students. There are now around 15,000 graduates and undergraduates, and the university is supported by 14 Commonwealth Caribbean countries. Just inside the main gates, on your right, is the chapel built from the stones of a ruined sugar warehouse on Gayle's Valley Estate in Trelawny.

The outer Ring Road (follow the directional signs) will take you past the faculties of Medicine, Engineering, Law, the Humanities, the Natural and Social Sciences and the Philip Sherlock Center for the Creative Arts before you come full circle to the main gates.

Retrace your route but continue past Wellington Drive and enter Hope Road where it joins with Mona Road. This is a very busy intersection and Jamaicans are not the most patient or courteous of drivers. Just beyond the traffic lights at Hope and Old Hope Road (left) is the main entrance to the newest and most attractive of Kingston's shopping complexes, the **Sovereign Center**, on your right. It's worth a detour through the shops if you are in the mood to browse. There is a food court and shops on the lower level, two cinemas on the upper level and more shops on the middle level.

From Sovereign, turn right on Hope Road. The next sight you will pass is the **Bob Marley Museum** (Monday, Tuesday, Thursday, Friday 9.30am–4.30pm, Wednesday, Saturday and public holidays 12.30pm–5.30pm, tel: 927 9152), on your right. The outer walls are

Bob Marley

decorated with paintings of Marley, his album covers and his children. It is a well-laid-out tour with the **Queen of Sheba** restaurant (Monday to Saturday, 7.30am–10pm) on the right as you enter. The accent is on vegetarian or 'ital' (salt-free) cooking and fresh juices. They also do chicken and fish dishes.

Marley bought the house in 1975 from Chris Blackwell of Island Records, who was instrumental in launching the career of Bob Marley & The Wailers. The souvenir shop – all souvenirs are of Marley – was originally the Tuff Gong record shop. Tuff Gong is Marley's own label and the studio was originally housed in the cottage at the back. That cottage now houses an exhibition hall with Marley memorabilia, as well as a 'Things From Africa' shop. The newest addition to the museum complex is a screening room or small cinema (seats 40) which shows videos of Bob Marley's rise and career, as well as ethnic movies such as *Malcolm X*, *Cry Freedom*, etc. It's a very interesting tour, particularly for fans of Marley, whose voice continues to float out from speakers in various rooms.

At the intersection with Lady Musgrave Road, ahead of you on your right, is the entrance to **Kings House**, official residence of the Governor-General. You can drive through the grounds for a peek at the house; if you want to do that, get in the right-hand lane before you get to the traffic lights. Just beyond the intersection and next to Kings House is **Jamaica House**, the official residence of the prime minister and, no – you can't drive through!

The entrance to **Devon House** (tours Tuesday to Saturday, 9.30am–5pm) is on the right as you approach the central traffic

Devon House was built in 1881

island and the lights at the corner of Waterloo and Hope Roads. Built in 1881 by Jamaican George Stiebel, this stately house was bought by the government in 1967, restored and refurbished in keeping with the original, and opened to the public. The craft shops in the quadrangle behind the house were formerly servants' quarters, the Grog Shoppe is in the old carriage house and 'The Brick Oven' was the former kitchen. You can have a light lunch on the **Coffee Terrace** (Sunday 10.30am–2.30pm; 10am–6pm every other day except Monday to 4pm and Friday to 7pm) while watching the activities in the quadrangle, or enjoy a more substantial meal under the huge mango tree outside the **Grog Shoppe** (Monday to Saturday noon–10pm for meals; drinks until midnight). Opposite the Grog Shoppe's terrace is the entrance to a more formal restaurant, **The Devonshire** (Monday to Friday lunch noon–3pm; dinner 6pm–10pm, tel: 929 7046). Reservations are advisable at The Devonshire and they have a dress code. The prices are reasonable, however, and it is worth the effort of dressing up.

End the day in the cool serenity of the hills. Take Trafalgar Road heading east to the lights at Lady Musgrave Road. Turn left and follow the road to East Kings House Road. Stay left at the roundabout on East Kings House Road and get in the right lane as you round the corner. Turn right on Barbican Road and get on the left side of the road for Jacks Hill Road. Continue straight up and follow the signs to **Ivor Guest House** (tel: 927 1460 and 977 0033). It is a wonderful place for afternoon tea, served on the verandah or the lawn. The mountains rise behind you, their tops often enveloped in mist, while the sun slides into the sea behind Kingston and the first lights twinkle on. At this distance, Kingston is transformed into a place of beauty. Ivor is open for lunch (noon–2pm), tea (around 3pm–4.30pm) and dinner (7pm–9pm). Reservations are recommended and they close for refurbishing each September.

6. Port Royal and Lime Cay

Walking tour of Port Royal, once headquarters of the Royal Navy; picnic on Lime Cay. Reserve a boat for a picnic on Lime Cay from Morgan's, tel: 924 8464/5 or 8148. If you wish, they will also prepare a picnic lunch for you, or you can have your hotel make one up instead. Take a good sun block, a hat, and a beach towel. There is not much to photograph on Lime Cay, unless you go underwater, so lock your camera in the trunk of the car after touring Port Royal. Books and a Walkman would be useful if you intend to spend the day in splendid solitude.

Exit Kingston via Mountain View Avenue (a very long and winding road) then turn left at the traffic lights by Windward Road. The dormitory suburb of Harbour View begins just before the roundabout. Turn right at the roundabout on to the Palisadoes, a narrow, 9-mile-long neck of land which encloses Kingston.

On the right as you travel is the **Maritime Training Institute**, a school for Caribbean seamen established with the help of the government of Norway. Next to it, sharing the same entrance, is the **Royal Jamaica Yacht Club**, a private club which welcomes bonafide members of other yacht clubs.

At the next roundabout continue straight on for about 3–4 miles. Presently, the road runs alongside a long brick wall behind which is the old Admiralty Coaling Station, known as the Old Coal Wharf and the site of occasional open-air reggae concerts. Beyond that is the old Royal Navy garrison quarters next to **Morgan's**, a small hotel with a marina. The naval dockyard, circa 1720s, is next to the present day entrance to **Port Royal**.

Drive into the main square or Muster Ground as it was called, and along Tower Street. There is a car park next to **St Peter's Church** (1725) where you can leave your car and continue on foot if you wish, using the route map (*page 32–33*).

St Peter's is the third parish church to be built here, the first having been destroyed in the earthquake of 1692 and the second by fire in 1703. Its brick walls were, unfortunately, covered with cement during the last restoration and scored to simulate stone

In the marina at Morgan's

Nelson stood here

blocks. The interior, however, is full of interesting architectural detail, historical plaques and monuments. In the churchyard is the grave of **Lewis Galdy**, a Frenchman who survived the 1692 earthquake in miraculous fashion. The story of his escape is engraved on the tombstone.

Most visitors to Port Royal head straight for **Fort Charles** and you can too, but the entire area can be explored on foot in a little over an hour. Fort Charles is an integral part of the history of Port Royal. Work was started on it less than a year after the English captured the island from the Spanish in 1655, and it subsided more than three feet in the earthquake 37 years later. Despite repairs and additions it has not changed much since the mid-18th century, and is one of the oldest and best preserved forts on the island. The best-known and most illustrious commander of Fort Charles was Admiral Lord Nelson, and the wooden platform known as **Nelson's Quarter-deck** was his lookout to sea. There is a guide appointed by the Jamaica National Heritage Trust to show you around, or you can tour it on your own.

Check out the **Maritime Museum** in the restored buildings which Lord Nelson occupied. The Historic Room was his office, and the Modern Room his living quarters. Another popular feature of the Fort, particularly with children, is the Royal Artillery Store (c 1888) which tilted on its present angle in the 1907 earthquake. It has been aptly christened the **Giddy House** — try walking across its floor and you will see why.

Retrace your steps to the street opposite the car park on Tower Street. Turn right on Cannon Street and left on Gaol Alley. The **Old Gaol**, restored, is an outlet for books and crafts. Every two to three months, evenings of poetry reading and music are held to standing-room-only crowds. Parts of the gaol are thought to pre-date the 1692 earthquake.

Drive the short distance back to Morgan's where you'll board a boat for a session of sun and swimming at **Lime Cay**. This small, scrub covered sandspit is very popular with Kingstonians at weekends, but during the week you could have it all to yourself. The boat will drop you off and return for you whenever you say. It's about a 10–15 minute trip each way.

At the end of the day, if you are groggy from the sun but ravenously hungry, choose from the selection of Kingston restaurants listed in the *Eating Out* section. Bon appétit!

There's no shortage of green in the Blue Mountains

7. The Blue Mountains

A day trip into the Blue Mountain range; Newcastle military training camp, Hollywell National Park for some incredible vistas, lunch at the Gap Cafe with the best coffee, bar none, afterwards. Return through Section to World's End, for a tour of Dr Ian Sangster's liqueur factory with an opportunity to sample the product and make purchases.

If you have a fear of heights and sometimes precarious mountain passes, then this tour is not for you. If you don't, and you love the mountains, then you will enjoy an unforgettable day and experience some of the most magnificent vistas imaginable.

The **Blue Mountains** are one of the least publicized parts of the island – apart from the coffee they produce – and few visitors would ever associate its climate and plant life with a tropical country. The Blue Mountains are thought, by geologists, to be the oldest part of the island. They believe that Jamaica and the neighboring islands are the tops of volcanic land-masses that erupted from the seas billions of years ago, and that the lower surrounding lands surfaced gradually over 30 million years ago.

Mountain man

Wear comfortable clothes and walking shoes; take along a sweater or jacket and, again, don't forget your camera! Make sure you have a full tank of gas before you leave town; there are no gas stations in the mountains. Although much of this route is paved and passable in dry weather, there are sections where the going is very rough and can be difficult during or immediately after heavy rains. If it's

42

Cemetery at Newcastle

raining and you are unde-
cided, put it off for another
day or ring Mrs Palomino
(tel: 997 3032) at the Gap.
She knows the mountains
and can advise you. If you
leave town around 9am
you can do the entire trip
and be back in town by
5pm in good weather.

Head for the mountains via Hope Road to Papine,
an open square. Bear left at the gas station and left again at the
end of the short road. This is the Gordon Town Road which leads
over a short bridge past the **Blue Mountain Inn**. Just past the wall
of the inn, two roads lead off left, right next to each other. Take
the second exit and follow this road for about 9 miles to **Irish
Town**, passing private homes, including Bellencita, home of the
late Sir Alexander Bustamante. His widow, Lady Bustamante, still
lives in the house here.

Newcastle, at an altitude between 3,500 and 4,500ft, is about
2½ miles further on. It is a military camp commanded by the Jamaica
Defence Force (JDF). The road runs right through the parade-
ground, known as the Major-General Sir William Gomm Square,
after its founder. He established the camp in 1841 in an attempt
to reduce the high death rate from yellow fever which occurred at
lower altitudes. You can park against the railings on the far side
of the parade, where the road continues to Hollywell Park. This is
a good place for photographs, particularly if the JDF recruits are
training. The army rents out cottages very cheaply about a mile
above the camp.

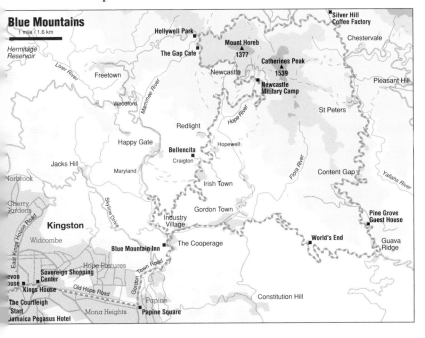

Mist shrouds a gateway in the Blue Mountains

Once out of the parade ground, the road is extremely narrow so proceed with care, using your horn. This is a thickly forested area with almost constant moisture in the air and the flowers and trees which grow here do not exist lower down the slopes. You will pass the **Gap Cafe & Gift Shoppe** first and you will be returning here for lunch. But drive on around the corner for the entrance to **Hollywell Park** and a quick tour of the facilities. The Park Ranger's cabin is on the right as you enter and picnic areas abound. The log cabins here can be rented from the Forestry Department at very reasonable rates. There are also several hiking trails, well marked, but if you follow them you won't have time for the rest of the itinerary.

Return to the Gap Cafe – the Fairy Glade hiking trail beckons across the road – for lunch. Eating in these surroundings could make you feel you never want to return to the city, and the food is excellent. If you are a coffee drinker, this is the

A splash of color

place to taste the *real* Blue Mountain coffee, supplied by a grower whose estate is a short distance away. The proprietor of the Gap is the afore-mentioned Gloria Palomino, a petite, energetic lady who, as Chairman of the Hollywell Conservation Trust, is very knowledgeable about the area.

After lunch, continue past Hardwar Gap to a junction with a signpost marked Section. Signs point in three directions: back the way you came, to Buff Bay on the north coast and, right, to Sil-

Blue Mountain Coffee

Coffee plants like lots of water, sloping well-drained soil, lots of shade when young and a cool climate. Consequently, they thrive in the mountainous terrain of Jamaica, growing at altitudes of between 1,500 and 5,000ft.

The coffee for which these mountains are famous was first brought to the island around 1728 by the then Governor of Jamaica, Sir Nicholas Lawes. He imported some berries and seedlings of the Cafe Arabica strain from Martinique, and planted them on his property at Temple Hall, St Andrew. It is from the Arabica variety (so called because coffee was discovered c14–15th century in Arabia where it is indigenous) that our Blue Mountain coffee is derived.

A certain mystique has developed around Blue Mountain coffee. Only on these slopes, it is claimed, does Arabica achieve *'the smoothness of texture, fullness of body, sweetness of taste and aroma that makes Blue Mountain coffee the best in the world.'*

Fortunately for us, the secret is one that is known only to Mother Nature.

ver Hill, St Peter's and Content Gap. Turn right towards Content Gap and about ¾ mile further on is a small road on the left, leading to the **Silver Hill Coffee Factory** which is signposted. Between September and February, you can see workers picking the red berries. They remove the outer red skin and wash off the gelatinous inner pulp (a process known as 'pulping') then spread the beans on a concrete apron, called a barbecue, for drying.

Just past Content Gap is the **Pine Grove Hotel** where, if you have time, you can stop for tea on the terrace. This is another great vantage point for photographs. Pine Grove also offers chalet-type accommodations, excellent Jamaican food and there is a bar in the main restaurant.

Follow the main road past **Guava Ridge** (junction with road to Mavis Bank) to **World's End** (tours Monday to Friday, 9am–4pm) where Dr Ian Sangster and his staff produce some of Jamaica's award-winning liqueurs and rums. You'll be given a guided tour and the chance to taste the products, purchases can after which be made in the gift shop.

From World's End, you are 15 minutes or about 5 miles from **Gordon Town**, the only town on this stretch. Gordon Town is notable as the site of Jamaica's first botanical garden, established in 1770 by Hinton East. Mr East introduced hundreds of foreign plants from as far away as China and many of his specimens readily adapted to the climate and soil of Jamaica. The original garden, unfortunately, no longer exists, but the plants thrive in gardens across the island.

The most precipitous part of the journey is over once you reach Gordon Town, and so are the panoramic views. I hope you will agree that it was a very worthwhile trip.

Don't leave without one

OCHO RIOS & PORT ANTONIO

8. Main Street, Ochie

Visit botanical gardens 600ft above Ocho Rios; window-shop and have lunch on Main Street; tour a 1,000-acre plantation in a jitney; dine by the waterfalls at The Ruins (tel: 974 2442 or 2789); dance at Silks or The Acropolis. Take your camera and extra film.

Coconut men in Ochie

Although **Ocho Rios** – or 'Ochie' as we Jamaicans refer to it – translates as 'eight rivers,' no such number of rivers exists here. The name is believed to be a corruption of the Spanish *Las Chorreras*, meaning 'the waterfalls.' Perhaps 'place of the waterfalls' might be more accurate as there are several in this area, including the most well known, Dunn's River Falls.

Ocho Rios had no particular claim to fame until it began its growth as a tourist resort 30 years ago. Since then, it has been busy shedding its over-worked description as 'a sleepy little fishing village.' Today it is the favored destination of visitors and Kingstonians who flock here on public holidays. Its central area of activity stretches away from the clock tower at the junction of Main Street and DaCosta Drive, along the coast road (the A3) in both directions, bounded roughly by Dunn's River Falls in the west and the White River in the east. Now bursting at the seams, a by-pass is currently being built to relieve the congestion of through traffic, particularly at the junction of DaCosta Drive and Main Street, the busiest intersection day or night.

Shaw Park Botanical Gardens give a fine view over Ocho Rios Bay

Another central point is the roundabout where Milford Road and DaCosta Drive intersect. Milford Road is the beginning of the main route leading up through Fern Gully and across the mountains to Kingston.

To get to the day's visit to **Shaw Park Botanical Gardens** (daily 9am–5.30pm) drive to the roundabout at Milford Road and DaCosta Drive. Turn uphill on Milford Road towards Fern Gully. It's a good idea to set out at around 9am before the sun gets too hot and the streets too crowded. About half a mile up this road and opposite St John's Anglican church is a small road on your right with a signpost to Shaw Park Gardens. Follow this road until just past the Shaw Park Dairy where the road forks; the left fork takes you up to The Ridge, an exclusive residential area. Take the right fork to the gardens.

The gardens were the site of an 18th-century Great House, which was subsequently converted into the Shaw Park Hotel. A fire devastated the hotel several years ago and it has been rebuilt as the Shaw Park Beach Hotel along the coast road next to the White River. At an elevation of 600ft, these informal gardens command an unparalleled view over Ocho Rios Bay. Wooden steps allow you to descend and ascend with ease to the various levels and lead to secluded areas, some of them beside streams and waterfalls. There is also a bird sanctuary and your guide can identify the different types for you. If you are inclined to linger, there is a nice shady bar where you can quench your thirst.

Waterfall in Shaw Park

Tangerines

Afterwards, return to the roundabout at the bottom of Milford Road, cross it, and continue to **Main Street** (a one-way street in an easterly direction). This is a lively little street with banks, a post office, the main office of the **Jamaica Tourist Board** (upstairs in Ocean Village Plaza), a supermarket, numerous restaurants and fast food outlets, as well as plazas in which to browse or shop while you work up an appetite. Parking on the street is very restricted but you can usually find space in the Ocean Village Shopping Center, opposite the post office and Scotiabank.

Between the cruise ship pier and the clock tower Main Street is easy to explore on foot and the shops and boutiques tend to be concentrated at the eastern end. Pick up a copy of *Ocho Rios & Beyond* at the Jamaica Tourist Board's office, or the Visitor Information booth on Main Street outside the Turtle Towers condominiums. It's a fold-out brochure put together by the merchants of the area, and the rough map in the center identifies places and helps you get your bearings.

The **Taj Mahal Plaza**, a replica of the Indian monument of the same name, is at the western end of this strip. It has several duty-free shops and there are more in the **Little Pub** complex further along Main Street. Some of the more interesting shops are in the **Ocean**

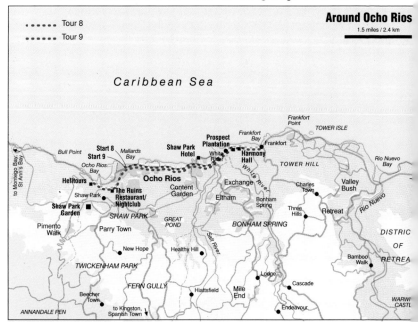

Around Ocho Rios

1.5 miles / 2.4 km

· · · · · Tour 8

▪ ▪ ▪ ▪ ▪ Tour 9

Village Shopping Center and Island Plaza opposite the craft market. Ocean Village Shopping Center shares the parking lot with the largest of the three **craft markets** in Ocho Rios. The other two are at Pineapple Place and Coconut Grove further east past the clock tower. Do not be afraid to haggle a little with the vendors. Most of them expect to negotiate and will enter into the spirit of it good-naturedly.

You're probably hot and tired by now, so head for Soni's Center (opposite the craft market) and the cool interior of **The Forever Cafe** (daily 6.30am–11.30pm). Their menu includes grilled steaks and lobster, sandwiches, salads, sodas, shakes, etc. and their prices are moderate. Alternatively, there are several fast-food places which are all within easy walking distance of each other on Main Street and nearby.

After lunch, drive past the clock tower, heading east across the White River towards **Prospect Plantation** (three tours daily; Monday to Saturday, 10.30am, 2pm, 3.30pm. Sunday, 11am, 1.30pm, 3pm. Children under 12 free). About a 10-minute drive. The entrance to the Plantation is on the right, shared with the Prospect Ice Factory. This 1,200-acre working plantation was established in the 1950s by the late British baronet and Member of Parliament, Sir Harold Mitchell. Sir Harold and Lady Mitchell lived in the Great House on the property which the tour passes, but it is not open to the public.

In the shade at Prospect Plantation

The tour of Prospect by tractor-drawn jitney takes about 1½ hours. Frequent stops are made to explain the sights and to allow you a close-up look at many of Jamaica's most important economic crops. You'll also have panoramic views over the White River gorge and from **Sir Harold's Lookout** over Ocho Rios from where, on a clear day, you can see Cuba.

There is a cadet training college on the estate, established by Sir Harold in 1956, from which many of the guides are drawn. The tour ends at the students' non-denominational **chapel**, an elegantly simple structure in a grove of flowering trees. The chapel is also open to the public and dates and times of services can be obtained from the estate office or from hotels in the Ocho Rios area.

If you wish, you can leave a permanent record of your visit by planting a tree which the estate guarantees to maintain. Pick up a copy of the leaflet with details at the central reception area. The plantation can also be toured on horseback, but you'll have to call at least an hour ahead to reserve horses. Three scenic rides are of-

Eating by the waterfall at The Ruins (see below)

fered, ranging from 1–2¼ hours' duration. There is also a mini 18-hole golf course for children and simulated clay-pigeon shooting with laser guns.

Round off your day at **The Ruins** (daily 6–9.30pm; lunch Monday to Saturday noon–2.30pm), a casually elegant restaurant where you can dine under the stars beside a waterfall in a tropical garden. The falls were originally used to turn mills for grinding sugar cane when the property was owned by one Robert Rutherford who built a great house here in the 1800s. When his marriage went sour, Rutherford moved to Montego Bay and the factory and plantation on this site fell into ruins – hence the name. The present restaurant was opened in 1982 and gained immediate popularity as much for its cuisine – Chinese and Jamaican – as for the beauty of its setting. A gift shop and boutique were added three years later. In high season (mid-December to mid-April) there is live music three times a week; the rest of the year there is background recorded music.

If you are still up for some fun after dinner try **Silks** in the Shaw Park Hotel. It's a small, pub-style disco, very popular with the older crowd as it is less noisy than most. Try to get there before 11pm if you want to rest your legs between dances, particularly at weekends. Younger disco fans, and the young at heart, gravitate to the high-tech Acropolis from midnight onwards, where they periodically have live performances by various artistes, fashion shows and events for beauty contestants.

Alternatively, if all you crave is a nightcap before turning in, a good place for just hanging out and reminiscing with tunes of yesteryear is the **Vintage Bar** (daily 10am–2am) on the roof of Soni's Plaza; vintage oldies recorded music plays until the last drop has been drunk. Friday night is *soca* (the music of carnival) oldies night and die-hard sports enthusiasts can keep track of all events via satellite TV. Alternatively, watch sports on TV at **Bill's Place**, upstairs at 47 Main Street; very popular with the avid sports crowd and the customers are pretty lively when a game is on.

9. Harmony, Heli, and Dunn's River

Art and Craft gallery with a difference; 'The Jamaican Showcase' helicopter tour across the island (book if possible, tel: (809) 974 1108, 974 1587 or 1588; Fax: (809) 974 2183, 974 1247); climb Dunn's River Falls; finish at The Little Pub dinner/theatre (reservations tel: 974 2324 or 5826). Take your swimsuit and towels for the falls. Leave any unnecessary jewelry behind.

Head east for **Harmony Hall** (daily 10am–6pm), a 10-minute drive from the clock tower, depending on traffic. A beautifully restored Victorian gingerbread house, it is deservedly the most popular art and craft gallery on the north coast. Harmony Hall is next to the Harmony Chalets on the right.

Harmony helpers

The gallery is on the upper floor and one of the rooms is reserved for the works of 'intuitive' or self-taught artists. Exhibitions change frequently and a variety of high quality craft and artwork is on sale, also books, posters and postcards. If you are lucky enough to be visiting when one of their craft fairs is being held (*see Calendar of Events*), try not to miss it. Entrance to the gallery and the fairs is free. The ground floor is occupied by a restaurant serving Jamaican cuisine.

My personal choice is to go next door to **Glenn's Jazz Club Restaurant** (9am until you say when), run by genial hosts Glenn and Madeline Whitter. Glenn Whitter is a jazz enthusiast and the background music is likely to be from his extensive collection of tapes, records and CDs. The restaurant is also one of the venues for performers during the annual Ocho Rios Jazz Festival (*see Calendar of Events*). On weekends – Friday or Saturday – you can catch live jazz performances. The company is convivial, the food is good, and the restaurant is very popular with locals and visitors.

Back-track through Ocho Rios, staying left of the clock tower on DaCosta Drive. Just beyond Reynolds bauxite wharf (recognizable by the red bauxite dirt covering everything) is the entrance to the Helitours helipad.

Helitours (Jamaica) Ltd is an Ocho Rios-based, tourist board licensed,

Harmony Hall

A helicopter's view of Ochie

helicopter tour and charter company, owned and operated by ex-Jamaica Defence Force officers, one of whom, Captain Tal Stokes, is a member of the Jamaica bobsled team. Each of their Bell Jet Ranger helicopters carries four passengers plus the pilot, who also gives a running commentary of the view below. (You are supplied with headphones so that you can hear the pilot's narration; it also helps to deaden the sound of the rotor blades.) The company offers a variety of tours, from the 15-minute 'Ocho Rios Fun Hop,' to an all-day island tour which you might want to try another day. The island tour is not cheap (currently US$2,100 for 1–4 people), but the all-inclusive price is well worth it. It is advisable to book as far in advance as possible, and at least a day before you wish to fly, as flights are scheduled on a first-come, first-served basis. For information and details of the various tours and services, telephone Helitours or stop in at their offices at 120 Main Street, Ocho Rios.

For today, I suggest 'The Jamaican Showcase,' an exhilarating one-hour ride which takes you south across the island, over St Ann's rolling pastures and farms, over the bauxite works of Moneague and Ewarton, through the Bog Walk Gorge carved deep in the mountains by the Rio Cobre, and over the southern plains of St Catherine and its capital, Spanish Town. The tour then loops over Port Royal (at the entrance to Kingston), and Kingston spreads away in front and on either side of you, nestled between the Blue Mountains and the sea. The return journey is through the Stony Hill gap in the mountains and over the eastern end of the north coast. You fly past Noel Coward's hilltop home, Firefly, as well as Golden Eye, retreat of the late Ian Fleming, and the place where he created the James Bond series, before you return to Ocho Rios.

Back on the ground, you are a short distance from **Dunn's River Falls** (daily 9am–5pm; when cruise ships are in they open 8am–5pm).

Dunn's River Falls: beware cold water!

Drive west along the coast road for about half a mile. The sign for the turn-off is on your left. Remember to lock your car and place any valuables in the trunk. Although there are lockers for storing your clothes, they are not reputed to be very secure. The parking lot is dotted with assorted snack bars, souvenir stands and arts and craft vendors.

It is traditional to climb the falls, and for that you have to buy a ticket and go down the stairs to the beach. The entrance fee is nominal and the falls are easy to climb on your own. Just take it slowly and check your footing. Alternatively, you might find joining one of the guided groups weaving up in a daisy chain more fun. On a very hot day the water can be positively icy and you might prefer to get acclimatized by a swim in the sea beforehand.

Round off your day at **The Little Pub** (Main Street, dinner 6pm–midnight), an institution in Jamaican entertainment for the past 25 years, due largely to the energy and innovation of proprietor Keith Foote. Many of the musical revues and cabaret shows presented here would not seem out of place off-Broadway and Keith Foote has a hand in writing and producing them all. The resident band provides background music while you dine, and you can dance afterwards until showtime at 10pm. This is a lively and entertaining venue with seating for 200.

10. To Port Antonio

This itinerary involves an overnight stay. To Firefly (daily 8am–6pm), home of late British playwright, Noel Coward; lunch and swim at Crystal Springs tel: 929 6280; visit to the rainforest/Somerset Falls; dinner and overnight at Bonnie View Hotel – reservations tel: 993 2752 or from the US (800) 448 5398. On the second day of this trip: early morning ride to Folly, lighthouse and beach; Rio Grande rafting with lunch at Betty Wilson's riverside canteen; Rafter's Rest by 4pm and start your trip to Ocho Rios.

Pack an overnight bag, your swimsuit, beach towel, camera and lots of film. It's a very scenic drive. A picnic basket with fruit/sandwiches/liquid refreshment is optional, but it might be handy for an impromptu stop

Drive carefully

if you become peckish on some of the longer stretches. A pocket knife for peeling fruit is always handy, and don't forget the sun block and a shady hat for the raft trip.

This itinerary takes you from the parish of St Ann, into St Mary and finishes up in Portland. The beauty of the coastline of St Mary and Portland conjures up a wealth of superlatives and you'll probably come up with a few of your own. The unhurried pace, the climate and the breathtaking scenery have lured writers, artists, movie stars and film crews here for many years. Parts of this entire stretch of coast have been location sites for such films as *Cocktail*, *Club Paradise*, *Clara's Heart*, *Papillon* and a host of others.

Port Antonio, Portland's capital town, is credited with being the cradle of two of Jamaica's major industries: tourism and bananas. The bananas are still here, but the majority of visitors seem to prefer the more hectic pace of Montego Bay and Ocho Rios, although these places cannot compete with Portland's serene beauty.

As you'll be traveling east, plan to leave between 9–10am, when the sun is well above the horizon, so you won't have to combat the glare directly in your eyes. The trip will take the best part of the day but can be accomplished comfortably in daylight.

From the roundabout, take the A3 (coast road) heading east across the White River which marks the boundary between the parishes of St Ann and St Mary. Follow the route map on p.55. The two major hotels you'll pass between Harmony Hall and Oracabessa both belong to the Superclubs chain: **Couples** (all-inclusive, and as the name suggests, for couples only), and **Boscobel**, just before the Boscobel aerodrome. The latter is one of only two hotels on the island which currently caters specifically for families with young children. Rio Nuevo, between the two hotels, is the site of England's last battle with the Spanish for possession of Jamaica.

Beyond Boscobel is the little village of Oracabessa (derived from the Spanish *ora* – gold, *cabeza* – head). You will notice that many of the places here have names beginning with 'gold' or 'golden.'

The late Ian Fleming's Golden Eye is nearby, just off the main road. It is now owned by Island Records mogul Chris Blackwell.

About 45 minutes from Ocho Rios is a blue and white fence and a sign proclaiming 'Blue Harbour.' Behind the fence is the house in which the late British playwright, Sir Noel Coward would put up his guests. His own house, **Firefly**, is about a minute away. Look for the sign, on your right, at the entrance to a narrow road. Proceed with care for about a mile up this road, using your horn as you approach the bends. Believe it or not, tour buses come up here and it's as well to announce your presence to other traffic from time to time. At the T-junction you will see a signpost pointing towards Firefly on the right, about half a mile further on.

Coward suffered a heart attack, died and is buried in the garden overlooking the sea. He left the property to a long-time friend

Henry Morgan, pirate

View from Firefly

and companion, who felt it rightly belonged to the people of Jamaica and handed it over to the Jamaican government. It was made a protected property under the stewardship of the National Heritage Trust Foundation (NHTF).

The house, outbuildings and grounds have been recently refurbished and landscaped by Chris Blackwell, who was himself born in St Mary and who has leased Firefly from the NHTF. He has painstakingly restored it to reflect, as accurately as possible, the way it was when Coward was alive. It's a small house and the guided tour lasts about 20 minutes.

The view overlooking Port Maria justifies the trip. In fact, Coward built a large open room to encompass this view, and composed a song about it: 'Room with a View'. It was his favorite place for entertaining and you'll understand why when you get there.

The property is said to have been owned originally by Jamaica's most well-known pirate, Henry Morgan, whom the British knighted as a reward for his assistance in their running battles with the Spanish fleet. The **Pirate's Kitchen** (so called because it is thought to have been Morgan's kitchen when he lived here) is in the small building next to the parking lot. It offers afternoon teas on the

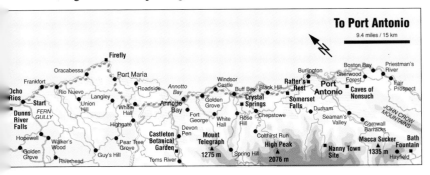

A perfect diet, waiting by the roadside

terrace, or you can simply sit at any time with coffee and pastries and enjoy the view. A bar, craft shop and toilet facilities are also in this building.

To get back to the main road, remember to turn left by the red water tank at the T-junction, and turn right at the bottom for Port Maria. The road hugs the coast here and the surface on this stretch is often pretty rough, despite attempts to keep it repaired, as it takes a pounding from the sea in bad weather, but the view is absolutely stunning.

A couple of outstanding 19th-century buildings, which are being restored, greet you as you enter **Port Maria**: St Mary's Parish Church (1861), on the left and, opposite, the old courthouse (1820). Like all market towns the streets are very crowded on traditional market days, usually Friday and Saturday. Keep to the left of the roundabout, exiting to the right through the town. Look for the yellow signpost by the roundabout if you become confused and follow the signs to Anotto Bay, Buff Bay and Port Antonio.

St Mary is the banana parish of the island and the road runs through numerous banana, and some coconut and citrus plantations. The blue plastic bags you'll see covering the bananas are to protect them from insects and birds.

A rasta shack offers silver colored cast-iron pots for sale at **Whitehall**, and if you have one of the old road maps, it will show 'Strawberry Fields' on the left near Albany, but this camping site and beach has now been renamed 'Sonrise.'

After Windsor Castle, the route becomes the A4 and **Buff Bay**, the next sizable town, is 10 miles away. Buff Bay is the old capital of what was once the parish of St George and you pass the 175-year-old St George's Anglican Church as you leave the town. Two and a half miles from Buff Bay a sign points to the road leading to **Crystal Springs**, 1½ miles inland.

This beautiful nature reserve and bird sanctuary (open daily 9am–6pm) is owned and managed by Jackie and Pauline Stuart. The nominal entrance fee entitles you to a guided tour of the property, use of the fresh water swimming pool and changing rooms, as well as giving access to the small folk museum. There are acres of gardens criss-crossed by streams, a water-wheel, an orchid garden and a small gift shop; there is even a conference room with support facilities located here.

The rustic log cabins have electricity and running water (no hot water) and are available for rent at very reasonable rates; alternatively, there is a campsite which is cheaper still. All meals are served in the open-sided restaurant, but reservations are advisable for breakfast and dinner. They can also cater for vegetarians if you indicate this when making reservations. You are welcome to picnic in the grounds provided no litter is left behind and the strict rules prohibiting open fires are observed.

Somerset Falls, just beyond Hope Bay, is another scenic spot. It is a former indigo and spice plantation with a spectacularly beautiful river gorge in a rain forest, with high waterfalls and deep pools for swimming. There is a small entrance fee, a restaurant and changing facilities if you wish to swim or take a boat ride to the 'Hidden Falls' in a secluded grotto.

Refreshing dip

From Somerset Falls, you are about 15 minutes from **Port Antonio**. A bridge crosses the Rio Grande next at **Rafter's Rest**. This is where you will return tomorrow in order to buy tickets for your rafting trip.

The A4 crosses the derelict railway lines and becomes West Palm Avenue as you turn left towards the center of Port Antonio. Thursday and Saturday are the main market days and this street is very crowded then. Continue to the T-junction with Street, facing the clock tower. Turn right on Street and right again on William Street. The road to Bonnie View is at an oblique angle to William Street, and is easiest to negotiate from this approach. The hotel is about a mile uphill.

The **Bonnie View** is a small, unpretentious, old-world hotel with just 20 rooms, which was built as a honeymoon retreat in 1943. The food is good, the staff friendly, and the view over the town and twin harbors is the best in the area. Book your horses for the ride to Folly next day, then relax with drinks on the terrace and ask the bar staff to tell you about the different places which can be seen from here.

Riding at Bonnie View

A Titchfield student

The following day, your guide will take you on an early morning ride to the ruins on **Folly Estate** and will tell you of the legend attached if you ask nicely; a round trip takes about 2½ hours or a bit longer if you decide to swim off Lighthouse Point. This is not a taxing ride, even for beginners, and there are some picture-perfect views of the Blue Mountains and Port Antonio. If you are not keen on horseback riding, Bonnie View offers a guided walking tour of the 22-acre plantation. Or you can drive or walk the short distance along Street to Titchfield Hill where the old barracks and parade grounds of Fort George have been converted into **Titchfield School**. You can walk around it (during school holidays), or tour the small streets to look at the gingerbread houses with a style of fretwork that has, unfortunately, gone out of fashion. One magnificent example of the period is the DeMontevin Lodge, circa 1898, at the corner of Fort George and Musgrave streets.

Check out of Bonnie View, lock your bags in the trunk of the car and drive to **Rafter's Rest**, an elegant building with a restaurant, bar, lounge area and washrooms. Purchase your tickets at the office here; each raft carries two people plus the raftsman, and the cost is per raft, not per person. A licensed and insured driver will take you to the starting point up river – either Grant's Level or Berrydale – and take your car back to Rafter's Rest to await your return.

The trip down river, from Grant's Level, takes a little over 3 hours; there could hardly be a more pleasant way to travel. If you feel the urge to swim at every likely spot, it will take longer. If you want to experience the river the Jamaican way, then stop at **Betty's riverside canteen** (about half-way downstream) and dine on soup made from janga (small river crayfish), or eat rice and peas with fried chicken, or ackee and saltfish with fried dumplings. Or try a little bit of everything.

Betty is personable, gregarious, and an excellent cook who has worked at some of the best hotels in Port Antonio. For the last eight years she has been performing amazing culinary feats in her little lean-to shack on the river bank; she has been featured in articles about the Rio Grande in the *New York Times*, and will happily recount for you the other publications in which she has been mentioned, as well as the list of well-known people who frequent her 'canteen' on a regular basis.

After the raft trip your drive back to Ocho Rios will take half as long, because you have seen some of the high spots on the way out and are now free to head straight back.

Shopping

When you think of shopping in Jamaica you'll probably think of duty-free bargains, straw goods and T–shirts. Well they are all here, but they are not even half the story.

You will be assailed by duty-free shops at every turn, all the resort areas have one or more craft markets, and there are vendors of everything from sea-shells to wood carvings along the roads. You won't have any trouble finding those. What you may find interesting are quality items that make great presents for friends or for yourself. Here are just a few suggestions:

Blue Mountain Coffee – roasted beans or ground coffee, in 1 or 2lb burlap bags, within a vacuum pack; also 1lb tins. Stocked in better supermarkets and gift shops.

Busha Browne's range of **gourmet products**, beautifully packaged and with tantalizing names such as Spicy Tomato Love Apple Sauce, Coffee and Rum Marmalade, Mint Pepper Jelly – and they taste good too! The range is found in better supermarkets as well as gift shops.

Walker's Wood jams, jellies, Jerk Seasoning and **Solomon Gundy**, a savory spread for toast or crackers. Available at supermarkets and gift shops.

Rums and Liqueurs: *Appleton Estate* and 12-year-old rums; *Tia Maria* coffee liqueur; *Sangster's Old Jamaica liqueurs* in very attractive stoneware containers. At most large resort supermarkets and liquor stores.

Exotic flowers to go: a box of exquisite tropical blooms and foliage (currently US$25) packed and ready to go. Order two days before departure. Tel: 953 2726 (Montego Bay) or 974 2201 (Ocho Rios).

Souvenir coins in gold, silver or boxed sets are readily available from the Bank of Jamaica, Souvenir Coin Department, Kingston.

Embroidery and cut-work linen and hand-painted items; **Original artwork** by internationally recognized Jamaican artists. From art galleries across the island.

Books: Jamaican recipes, art and photography – Ray Chen's book *Jamaica, The Beauty & The Soul* is a real

Essential items of headwear

pictorial keepsake; also novels by Jamaican authors.

Clothing: Jamaican designers are chic and innovative. Beautiful and practical outfits are available in cotton, linen and soft fabrics for evening wear. Batik silk and cotton items.

The following is not a complete list of shops, but it will give you a start and you are certain to find many other interesting places on your own.

Kingston

The Craft Cottage
Village Plaza, Constant Spring Road
Craft shops in Devon House
Corner of Waterloo and Hope Roads
Xaymaca
16 Waterloo Road
Patoo Gallery
Manor Park Plaza
The Wanderer
3 Queensway
The New Kingston Shopping Center
Dominica Drive
The Sovereign Shopping Center
Hope Road at Matilda's Corner.
There is an entire row of shopping malls on either side of Constant Spring Road, between South Avenue and Half Way Tree

Ocho Rios

Ocean Village Shopping Center, Island Plaza, Coconut Grove
All on Main Street
Harmony Hall
Main road, 4 miles east of Ocho Rios

Montego Bay

Miranda Ridge
Gloucester Avenue
Things Jamaican
44 Fort Street
Budhai's Studio and Gallery
Reading
Montego Bay Craft Market

Cloth dolls

Eating Out

Good food is one of life's great pleasures and here, in Jamaica, you can practically dine your way around the world's cuisines. That is not as boastful a claim as it may seem. Remember that, although we are all Jamaicans, we are a nation of many races and we all brought our varying dishes with us. Indigenous Jamaican cuisine is a smooth blend of African, European and Oriental influences.

There are a few dishes worthy of special mention, partly because they are very good, and partly because you are bound to encounter them.

Ackee and saltfish: there is some controversy about whether the ackee is a fruit or a vegetable. Whatever, it was brought here from Africa and is eaten as a vegetable. When cooked the yellow inner pod disintegrates very easily and looks a bit like scrambled eggs if it is allowed to become too soft. It is highly seasoned and cooked with salted cod (saltfish) and is very popular as a breakfast, lunch or even supper dish.

Ackee & Saltfish

Patties: this is our version of the English pasty. A filling, usually meat, is highly seasoned and wrapped in a flaky pastry crust, then baked. It is eaten hot, never cold. The filling can be made from flaked lobster meat, shrimp, chicken or vegetables, usually *calalloo*, a type of spinach. Patties are Jamaica's first fast-food, popular before hamburgers and hot dogs became widespread. **Tastee** in Kingston and **Butterflake** in Montego Bay make some of the best patties in the island.

Rice and peas: this traditional Sunday dish is made from red kidney beans, not peas. It can also be made with Congo or gungo peas, black-eye peas or cow peas. The dried beans or peas are first cooked in coconut milk to which seasonings have been added – escallion, thyme, perhaps a small piece of salt pork – and the rice is added to this mixture when the beans or peas are half cooked. This is served as an accompaniment to the main meat dish, usually a roast of some sort.

Plantains: not to be confused with bananas, although they look like them, but are larger. You could say they are cousins to the banana but that is where all resemblance ends. They cannot **ever** be eaten uncooked, even when ripe: apart from having an unpleasant taste raw, they will give you the worst case of indigestion you could imagine. When fried or boiled, however, the transformation is nothing short of magical. Deliciously sweet.

Bammy and festival: the first is a flat sort of bread made from the cassava, a root vegetable. It is baked or fried and is excellent with fried fish. Festival is a kind of dumpling (made from cornmeal, flour, salt and a raising agent) which is fried; also good with fried fish and other meats.

Jerk – pork, chicken or fish: *jerk* refers to the method of cooking, a style inherited from the days of the buccaneers, when they used to cook meats over an open fire on a grill made from wooden twigs. The original jerk pork came from Boston in Portland. A pit is dug in the ground and a fire is built in the bottom. A lattice work grill of pimento (allspice) twigs is laid across the mouth of the pit. The pork, beaten flat and seasoned (highly, of course) is laid across the twigs. More twigs and pimento leaves are laid on top of the meat and then a sheet of zinc on top of that. The meat is then left to cook. The pimento wood and leaves lend a wonderful aromatic flavor to the meat as it cooks.

The whole business of jerk cooking has taken off, and there are pan-cooked meats available at almost every street corner in Kingston as soon as it becomes dusk. Naturally, no one has the time to run around looking for pimento leaves and twigs, but the berries used in the seasoning produce much the same effect.

My recommended Jamaican restaurants follow overleaf. As a rough guide to what you might expect to pay for a meal, without aperitifs, wine or dessert, venues have been categorized as follows: **$** = under US$5 and up to US$10; **$$** = over US$10 and up to US$20; **$$$** = US$20 and over. Prices are per person.

Fish and festival, a sort of fried dumpling made from cornmeal

Kingston

BLUE MOUNTAIN INN
Gordon Town Road
Tel: 927 1700 or 2606
Lunch and dinner. Romantic setting for dinner and the food is excellent. Continental. **$$$**

By the Blue Mountain Inn

IVOR
Jacks Hill
Tel: 927 1460, 977 0003
Lunch, afternoon tea, dinner. Local and continental dishes. Reservations required. **$$$**

STRAWBERRY HILL
Irish Town
Tel: 944 8400/7
Dine in a Blue Mountain setting, with spectacular views. A favorite spot for Sunday brunch with Kingstonians. **$$$**

GORDON'S RESTAURANT
36 Trafalgar Road
Tel: 929 1390
Lunch and dinner. Korean, Japanese and Chinese cuisine. Very good. **$$**

HEATHER'S GARDEN RESTAURANT
9 Haining Road
Kingston 5
Tel: 926 2826
Open daily for lunch and dinner. Attractive setting, generous portions, several Syrian dishes as well as seafood and Jamaican. **$$**

CARLOS' CAFE
22 Belmont Road
Kingston 5
Tel: 926 4186
Open daily for lunch and dinner. Italian, seafood and Jamaican menu. **$$**

REDBONES – THE BLUES CAFE
21 Braemar Avenue
Tel: 978 8262
Good food accompanied by jazz or blues music. **$$**

HOT POT
2 Altamont Terrace
New Kingston
Tel: 929 3906
Jamaican menu. Always busy, a good sign. Open 8am–10pm. **$**

MINNIE'S ETHIOPIAN HEALTH FOOD RESTAURANT
176 Old Hope Road
Kingston 6
Tel: 927 9207
Hearty vegetarian meals with an African flavor; natural fruit juices. Open 8am–10pm. **$**

GLORIA'S
Port Royal
Open daily. Great fried fish, bammy and festival. There are two outlets, both rustic but popular. **$**

Montego Bay

Most of these restaurants offer free transportation (for dinner, usually) from hotels.

TA-KE JAPANESE RESTAURANT
At the Sea Shell Inn
Mabel Ewin Drive
Tel: 979 9816
Jamaica's only Japanese restaurant. Lunch and dinner only. Freshly made sushi to order, Teppan-Yaki and Tempura cuisine. They offer free pick-up from your hotel. **$$$**

THE GEORGIAN HOUSE
2 Orange Street
Downtown Montego Bay
Tel: 952 0632
Dinner only. Elegant service in an 18th-century building. Continental. $$$

RICHMOND HILL INN
Off Union Street
Tel: 952 3859
Lunch and dinner. Elegant, superb setting. Good broiled lobster with drawn butter (in season). Continental. $$$

NORMA AT THE WHARF HOUSE
Reading
Tel: 979 2745
Tuesday through Saturday. Elegant dining by the sea. Innovative and delicious Jamaican cuisine. $$$

DOLPHIN GRILL
Holiday Village
Rose Hall
Tel: 953 2676
Coffee shop and outdoor dining. Local and international. Good food. Limousine service for 4 or more. $$

THE PELICAN
Gloucester Avenue
Tel: 952 3171
Good food, fast, efficient service. Local menu. Breakfast is a Montego Bay institution. Lunch and dinner too. $$

THE PORK PIT
Gloucester Avenue
Tel: 952 1046
Open from lunch-time through dinner. Casual, open air. Jerked meats and fish. $$

Ocho Rios
THE ALMOND TREE RESTAURANT
Hibiscus Lodge,
Tel: 974 2813
Open daily. Extensive menu. $$–$$$

CARIB INN RESTAURANT
Just past the clock tower on Main Street
Tel: 974 2445
Seafood is their specialty; also continental and local cuisine. $$–$$$

THE FOREVER CAFE
Soni's Plaza
Main Street
Breakfast, lunch and dinner. Good selection of steaks, sandwiches, salads. $–$$

THE PARKWAY
DaCosta Drive
Breakfast through dinner. Popular stop for the tour bus operators. Service is patchy but there are good local specialties. $–$$

DOUBLE V JERK CENTER
East of Ocho Rios on the left of Main Street, past Hibiscus Lodge
Not open on Sunday. Spicy jerk pork and chicken. Popular, lively hangout. $–$$

THE ORIGINAL BLUE CANTINA
Main Street
Tel: 974 2430
Mexican food, also hamburgers and very long hot-dogs. $–$$

Beware the kick of the punch

Nightlife

Nightlife in the resort areas centers around a reggae beat, limbo dancing and fire-eating. There are alternatives, however, when you have tired of the spectacle. Most of the larger hotels put on creditable shows giving exposure to some formidable local talent, particularly the singers. There are evening cruises on ketches and catamarans, torch-lit boat rides along the river for dinner and entertainment, and there are bars where you can just have a drink and listen to music, or dance if you choose.

Kingston

For an exposure to the variety of talent and culture of Jamaicans, however, Kingston is the place to be. Kingston is where you will find the National Dance Company (NDTC), the Jamaica Philharmonic Symphony Orchestra, the National Chorale, and every type of theatrical performance, from the bawdy to the esoteric. Several cinemas offer the latest releases, discos abound in the capital city and you can dance the night away every night if you choose. For a look at what's happening and where, check the entertainment pages of the local newspapers. Some popular Kingston night spots are:

Cultural show on stage in the Ward Theater, Kingston

The Greendale community advertises its night of Revelation

MINGLES
In the New Courtleigh Hotel
Knutsford Blvd
Particularly lively on weekends.

PEPPERS
On Upper Waterloo Road
An after-work bar with recorded music and occasional live performances.

24KT
In the Manor Center
Constant Spring Road
One of the more recent restaurants-cum-nightclubs; occasionally has fairly avant garde entertainment.

GODFATHERS
69 Knutsford Boulevard in the center of New Kingston
Another very popular nightclub/disco. Karaoke singing is the big thing here and they also have live performances.

Montego Bay

THE CAVE
Seawind Hotel
Montego Freeport
MoBay's most popular disco with music until the wee hours of the morning.

PIER 1
Howard Cooke Boulevard, right on the waterfront
This very popular nightspot has well-attended Friday night sessions which begin as soon as the sun has gone to bed. Open until late.

Ocho Rios

ACROPOLIS
Main Street
This is the current in-place with the lively disco crowd. Good blend of music and also the venue for frequent live events.

Tunes for tourists

LITTLE PUB
Main Street
Their resident band plays every night. Their musical revues are well produced and entertaining. There is a cover charge if you are not dining.

SILKS
In the Shaw Park Hotel
Is popular with residents who like the informal pub-style atmosphere and good dancing music.

Calendar of Special Events

JANUARY

Little Movement (**LTM**) **National Pantomime** (Ward, Kingston) Annual Jamaican musical opens on Boxing Day (December 26) for a 2- to 3-month run. It has become a traditional part of the Christmas season since its inception over 50 years ago. Showcases the best of Jamaican playwrights, musicians, actors/actresses, producers and directors. Contact: Jamaica Tourist Board offices worldwide.

Jamaica School of Dance Concert Season (Little, Kingston) end of January. An annual season of creative dance based on Caribbean movements and themes. Contact: Little Theatre, tel: 926 6129.

FEBRUARY

LTM National Pantomime (February to April, Little Theatre, Kingston). If you missed it at the Ward, here's your chance to catch it in uptown Kingston.

Pineapple Cup/Montego Bay Yacht Race (Montego Bay Yacht Club). This 81-mile race begins in Miami, goes around the Bahamas and the eastern tip of Cuba, and finishes in

The Jamaica School of Dance at the Little Theatre

Montego Bay. Lots of festivities at the Yacht Club during and at the end of the race. Contact: Patrick O'Callaghan, tel: 979 8038.

Sugar Cane Ball, Round Hill, tel: 952 5150. Annual charity ball, very formal, very grand, in aid of Hanover charities.

Polo match

Bob Marley Birthday Bash (Bob Marley Museum, Kingston, tel: 923 9380/2/4). Annual celebration of Marley's birthday, February 6, ending with a concert featuring Rita Marley and some of Marley's children.

The **Jamaica Music Industry (JAMI) Awards** (Jamaica Pegasus Hotel, Kingston). Annual music awards presented in categories such as reggae, folk, gospel, jazz and classical. Guest performers. Contact: Anthony Gambrill, tel: 926 4500.

The Annual Gibson Relays (National Stadium, Kingston). Over 20 years of excellence in track and field sports with overseas and Jamaican competitors. Check the local newspapers for dates and times of events.

Cricket February and March are the high points of the cricket season in the West Indies with regional competitions and test matches, some of which are played at Sabina Park in Kingston. Also one-day cricket matches. Check the local newspapers and radio stations for details of dates and times.

Jamaica Polo Association's annual tournament (Chukka Cove, St Ann). Contact: Danny Melville, tel: 974 2593/2239.

Jamaica Polo Association Tournament & Horse Show (Chukka Cove, St Ann). Combined event with top riders from Jamaica, the US and European grand prix circuits.

Easter Craft Fair (Harmony Hall, Ocho Rios). The first of Harmony Hall's very popular annual craft fairs, held over the Easter weekend. Lively, interesting and a very social event. Tel: 975 4222.

Easter is also **Carnival** month in Jamaica. Events islandwide begin on Easter Monday and culminate with a grand costumed street parade in Kingston the following Sunday. Lots of individual fêtes (*soca* dance parties) at different venues, kiddies parade, reggae/calypso tents. Live bands from Jamaica and Trinidad, thousands of revelers take to the streets on Ole Mas' Sunday. Contact: JTB offices worldwide.

Carnival mask

Easter Regatta (Montego Bay Yacht Club). Contact: Patrick O'Callaghan, tel: 979 8038.

University Singers Concert Season (The Philip Sherlock Center for the

Creative Arts, Mona, Kingston). Begins the last week in April; weekly performances through May. Contact: The Philip Sherlock Center for the Creative Arts, tel: 927 1047.

MAY / JUNE

St James Horticultural Society Show (Montego Bay). Very popular annual exhibition with demonstrations, plant and refreshment sales. Contact: Ms Merle Dixon, tel: 952 4700.

Negril Carnival, Negril. Triathalon, float parade, concerts, Jamaica Police Band, *soca* parties (the word *soca* is a combination of soul and calypso. It is used to describe the music associated with carnival), *mento* bands (*mento* is Jamaica's folk music and a forerunner of reggae. The name describes not only the music but also the words and dance steps that go with it). All forms of cultural activities take over Negril in May. Contact: Sonia Gilpin, tel: 957 4473.

The Ocho Rios Jazz Festival started a few years ago with an after-noon of music in the grounds of the Carib Inn, Ocho Rios. It has since expanded to include international performers from Europe, Japan, the US and other Caribbean islands, performing alongside Jamaica's best. All sorts of events and venues. Contact: JTB offices worldwide, or the Jazz Hotline, tel: 927 3544.

JULY / AUGUST

Jamaica/America Fourth of July celebrations. A series of events planned by the United States Embassy and usually well supported. Contact: USIS, tel: 929 4850.

The big annual event this month and for the past few decades has been **Reggae Sunsplash**. In 1993, the event moved to Jamworld park, Portmore, Kingston and now events are held at locations on the island. Sunsplash has gone international, taking the acts on the road overseas, and bringing some overseas artists here for the traditional August bash. It's big and it's popular. **Contact**: JTB offices worldwide, or

Carnival arrives in Negril in May every year

National Hero Paul Bogle (see October)

is even a canoe competition for fishermen and some mind-boggling catches have been made from these craft.

There is a lot of socializing at the day's end during the marlin tournament, with festivities planned for the rest day and the final trophy awards' presentation day. Contact: Joe Kieffer or Paul Passmore, c/o the Port Antonio Marina, tel: 993 3209.

Golfers generally come into their own in the cooler months of the year, starting with the **Jamaica Open and Pro-Am** at the Wyndham/Rose Hall championship greens. Contact: The Jamaica Golf Association for precise dates, tel: 925 2325.

The Jamaican-German Society is very active and vibrant. They host their annual **Oktoberfest**, held at their headquarters in Kingston. It's a fun do with dancing, games, stalls, beer-drinking contests, and German and Jamaican dishes. Contact: Herman Tobisch, tel: 927 8207.

the promoters, Synergy, tel: 942 9115.

Not to be confused with Sunsplash is **Reggae Sumfest** held at the Bob Marley Center, Montego Bay. Created to fill the gap left by Sunsplash's move to Kingston, it offers similar entertainment with many of the acts appearing at both events. Contact: JTB offices worldwide.

OCTOBER

The main events this month center around the celebrations of **National Heroes Day** weekend and the annual marlin fishing tournament in Port Antonio. For a list of events over National Heroes Day weekend, contact the Jamaica Cultural Development Commission (JCDC), tel: (809) 926 5726, or the offices of the JTB.

Port Antonio's Annual International Marlin Tournament is one of the oldest and most prestigious sports fishing tournaments in the Caribbean, and is the culmination of the marlin season (roughly August to October). Overseas and Jamaican anglers compete in everything from powerful ocean-going yachts to smaller craft. There

NOVEMBER / DECEMBER

Panasonic – The Championships. Local golfers tee off at Sandals Golf & Country Club, Upton. Contact: The Jamaica Golf Association for details, tel: 925-2325.

The Montego Bay Yacht Club hosts the **Jamaica-America Cup Yacht Race** this month. Qualifying eliminations are held all over the United States; there are also workshops and speed clinics. Contact: Patrick O'Callaghan, tel: 979 8038.

The Johnny Walker Golf Championship is hosted at Tryall Golf and Country Club, Montego Bay, usually in mid-December. Dates are posted on a large sign at the entrance to Tryall; check announcements in the local newspapers and on radio, or contact the Tryall Golf and Country Club direct, tel: 956 5660/7.

Practical information

A fine way to arrive

BEFORE YOU ARRIVE

You can save yourself a lot of aggro with some advance planning. If you are not part of a tour group, you need to know how to get from the airport to wherever you plan to stay, particularly if your flight is delayed and you arrive in the middle of the night. You also need to know where you can change your money into the local currency before you leave the airport premises, for tipping baggage handlers or taxicab drivers.

An experienced travel agent should be able to answer these and other questions beforehand, or the nearest Jamaica Tourist Board office (see the list of Tourist Board contacts which appears on page 84) can give you up-to-date advice and information. The JTB will send you, free of cost, lists of hotels and guest houses in the areas you plan to visit, as well as brochures and current information.

GETTING THERE

By Air

Most travelers enter Jamaica through one of the two international airports – Donald Sangster International, Montego Bay, or Norman Manley International, Kingston. Several international airlines serve the island, including Air Jamaica, and numerous charters from North America and Europe.

By Sea

These are the main cruise lines which currently stop at Jamaica's ports:

Carnival Cruises, 1-800-327 9501
Costa Cruises 212-682 3505
Hapag Lloyd Cruises 312-332 0090
Holland America 1-800-223 6655
Home Lines 1-800-221 4041
K-Lines/Hellenic 1-800-223 7880
Norwegian Caribbean 1-800-327 7030
Paguet Line 1-800-221 2160/2490
Royal Caribbean Line 1-800-327 6700
Royal Cruise Lines 415-788 0601
Royal Viking Line 1-800-227 4246
Sun Line 1-800-223 5760

TRAVEL ESSENTIALS

Visas & Passports

Everyone is required to have a valid passport and a return or onward ticket, although US and Canadian citizens can travel with a voter's registration card, naturalization papers (id card) or a birth certificate. However re-entry into North America is virtually impossible without a passport. Check with the authorities in your own country for the regulations and for any health clearances you may need.

What to Pack

Lightweight summer clothing is fine year-round as there are no wild fluctuations in temperature, although there are significant differences between the coastal plains and the mountains. For trips into the mountains, sturdy walking shoes (non-slip soles) or sneakers are essential and a sweater or jacket to ward off the cooler air, especially when the sun goes down.

On the coast, light summer wear is suitable, but while swimwear is fine on the beaches or at poolside, you may attract unwanted attention on the streets, or may be refused entry into restaurants and shops. This goes double for business districts, and is just not done in Kingston.

Electricity

Most of the country operates on 110 volts/50 cycles, but some of the larger hotels use 220 volts or can provide adapters or transformers. It will still be 50 cycles, however, not 60, and some appliances may run slowly and/or overheat. The adapters will not solve this problem.

Customs

It is simpler to list what you can bring into the country than what you can't. These are: your personal belongings, 25 cigars, 200 cigarettes, one pint of liquor (excluding rum) 1/2lb of tobacco and one quart of wine. Everything else is either strictly prohibited or requires a mind-boggling amount of form-filling. If you have friends here and want to bring them a gift, double check with the nearest Jamaican consulate or embassy to avoid having it confiscated or being charged a horrendous amount of duty when you arrive.

Most of your questions about what you are allowed to take out can be answered by calling the Norman Manley International airport in Kingston: 924 8310; Sangster International, Montego Bay: 952 4567. Generally, US citizens can leave with US$600 worth of duty-free goods after a 48-hour stay, and family members can combine exemptions. If you are over 21 years of age, you may take 2 litres of alcoholic beverage, providing one is locally manufactured. Duty will be charged above this quantity. You can mail an unlimited number of gifts back to the States, free of US duty, provided they don't exceed US$25 worth to one person in a day. Exceptions to this rule are perfume, cigars, cigarettes and liquor; you cannot mail a duty free parcel to yourself. These gifts will not affect the US$600 exemption.

Canadian citizens are allowed C$25 worth of goods free of Canadian duty after a stay of 48 hours. After seven days stay, goods worth C$300 can be taken back, duty free, once in each calendar year. Freeport stores will mail your purchases.

Pets

Jamaica is free of rabies and has very stringent rules about pets entering the country. Only animals born and bred in the United Kingdom are allowed entry.

The Jamaican flag

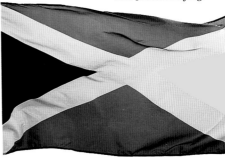

Departure Tax

This is levied on everyone leaving the island and is currently J$500. The amount is subject to change from time to time, depending on the stability of the Jamaican currency.

CLIMATE

The high season is mid-December to mid-April for the very good reason that, like birds, everyone likes to go south for the winter. Average temperatures throughout the year, along the coastal plains, range between 20°C–32°C. In the hills it can be 7–10°C lower and at the top of Blue Mountain peak, the highest point, temperatures have been known to drop below 10°C, but only rarely.

The weather can be unpredictable

The coolest months are November through April and the rainiest are May to June and September to October. Average rainfall annually is around 77 inches but Portland, the wettest parish, often gets four times that amount.

Hurricanes: The hurricane season officially begins in June and runs through to September, but in the last 40-odd years the island has only received three direct hits. Jamaica is linked to the US National Hurricane Center in Miami, Florida, which is equipped with sophisticated detection and tracking equipment, so early advice and warnings are the norm. Additionally, Jamaica's Office of Disaster Preparedness and Emergency Relief Coordination (the ODP) issues frequent broadcasts and advice on what steps to take should the island be in line for a direct hit.

GETTING ACQUAINTED

Jamaica is 146 miles long and 56 miles at its widest point. The country is bisected lengthwise by a mountain range which reaches its highest peak (7,402 feet) in the eastern Blue Mountain range. It is situated 600 miles south of Florida, or 1 1/2 hours' flying time from Miami.

Jamaica is an independent country, a member of the British Commonwealth of nations, and is a parliamentary democracy. The Queen is titular head of state, represented by a Governor-General whose powers are largely ceremonial. There are currently two major political parties: the People's National Party (PNP) and the Jamaica Labor Party (JLP).

Political power lies with parliament, headed by the prime minister from the ruling party, and consisting of a house of elected members (the house of representatives) representing 60 constituencies, and a senate of 21 members. Fourteen members of the senate are nominated directly by the prime minister and eight by the leader of the opposition.

The major contributors to the economy are bauxite mining, agriculture, tourism, and manufacturing.

Most religious denominations are represented in Jamaica. The major ones are Anglican (Church of England), Catholic, Baptist, Church of God, Methodist, Presbyterian and Seventh Day Adventists. Others include those of the Jewish faith, Hindus, Muslims, Baha'is and Rastafarians. There are more churches per square mile in Jamaica than anywhere else in the world, and the oldest Anglican cathedral in the western world is also to be found here, in Spanish Town.

The majority of Jamaicans are of African descent, creating a largely black population with a smaller proportion of mixed African, Oriental and European ancestry, producing varying shades of skin color ranging from darkest black to palest cream, and everything in between. Nowhere else in the Caribbean have the races melded so successfully nor, for the most part, so harmoniously, in turn giv-

A mixed race...

ing rise to the national motto: 'Out of Many, One People.'

Jamaicans for the most part are a very resourceful people, adept at devising strategies to circumvent unforeseen difficulties and challenges. They are highly individualistic and entrepreneurial and resent being patronized, particularly on their own turf. They are especially allergic to being referred to as 'natives,' and while most will pose for photographs, they prefer to be asked beforehand.

Jamaica is the largest English-speaking island in the Caribbean although you may find this difficult to believe from listening to the language on the street. It's a long story, but it can be summarized fairly quickly. Remember the Spanish bringing the first Africans here? The Africans came from different countries and tribes, speaking different languages and dialects. Then came the British, from all over the British Isles, with their regional dialects and intonations. They had to communicate with the Africans who, in turn, learned English from them, complete with inflections and varied pronunciations. Add to this mélange the later arrivals: the Middle-Easterners, Orientals, and other European peoples. The common language was English, but with words, inflections and grammar incorporated from each, the whole overlaid on a base of numerous African languages and – hey presto! You have 'Jamaica Talk'. It's English sure enough, but not as you will ever hear it spoken anywhere else.

Rastafarians have devized their own vocabulary, some of which has crossed over into common use due to the influence of reggae. The personal pronoun 'I' is central to Rasta terminology and is used as a prefix in many words, eg: 'I-dren' = brethren, 'I-and-I' or 'I-man' = me or myself. 'Dread' as an adjective means awful or rough as in, 'It dread out dere,' referring to the cost of living.

MONEY MATTERS

Legally, the only official currency is the Jamaican dollar, and it should be used everywhere, except for the purchase of duty-free goods. Exchange bureaus (6.30/

...living harmoniously together

7am–10.30pm, later for delayed flights or special charters) are in both international airports in the transit lounges and before you leave customs and immigration, or you can change your currency at one of the commercial banks. You will be given a receipt which you will have to present at the end of your stay if you want to re-convert your Jamaican money. Do not, however, convert all your money at once because you can only redeem a portion (currently US$200) when you leave. You can also change your currency at the hotels but check their rates against those of the commercial banks first.

Black Market Dealers

There is a thriving black-market despite the government's efforts to stamp it out, and you will be approached frequently. One of the problems you may encounter if you go this route is the inability to convert your Jamaican currency when you are ready to depart. The other is the possibility of counterfeit money.

Traveler's Checks and Credit Cards

Most major credit cards are accepted and traveler's checks can be used throughout the island. In banks you will be asked for identification, and your passport or travel document will suffice. Most commercial banks offer cash advances against credit cards. Jamaica Citizens and National Commercial banks offer advances against Mastercard and Visa, available at any of their branches island-wide. You can also get cash through any Western Union office (toll free 991 2057).

For lost or stolen traveler's checks or credit cards see Useful Addresses, page 83.

Tipping

A service charge is normally added to bills in restaurants, but if in doubt, feel free to ask. The norm is usually between 12–15 percent of the bill. Tipping of tour guides is not obligatory but is much appreciated, if you feel they are deserving.

HUSTLERS AND FREELANCE GUIDES

You are undoubtedly going to encounter hustlers trying to sell you something or, if you are lost, to accompany you and show you the way to where you are going. The problem with the latter is that they are often parasites, hoping to assign themselves the job of tour guide/companion for the duration of your stay. These hustlers are known locally as 'rent-a-dread' (short for dreadlocks; another name for Rasta is dread). They usually affect the Rasta dreadlocks or use Rasta idiom freely in their speech. The true Rasta would consider such parasitical behavior totally beneath his dignity.

If you are not interested in the hustlers' goods or services, just say 'no thank you' politely but firmly. If the hustling becomes a hassle, look around for the nearest policeman. A few people will genuinely assist you if you are lost and will be mortally offended if you offer money, but your good judgment should enable you to sort out who's who.

GETTING AROUND

Taxis from the Airport

If you are not part of a charter group or are not being met, you should check with the jtb or Visitor Information desk (there is one in each of the international airports) in the terminal, tell them your destination and ask what a reasonable fare should be from the airport. Once you get out of the terminal, you'll most likely be rushed by a flock of taxi drivers, hustling for fares.

Taxis are not metered, so strike a bargain with the driver of the cleanest, most roadworthy looking vehicle before allowing your luggage to be loaded.

From your Hotel

Check the best way to the airport with the front desk or tour desk staff.

On the Road

Always determine the fare with the driver before you get in. Once you've taken a few taxis, you'll begin to get an idea of what is reasonable and what is not. If you plan to use taxis as your mode of transportation and you find a driver that you like, it will save you a lot of haggling if you do a deal with him for the duration of your stay. Drivers often they make very knowledgeable guides, particularly in the resort towns.

Public versus Private Transportation

Public transportation is not for the faint-hearted. Buses are overcrowded, the service is irregular, the drivers treat the road like an autocross meet, and often devise their own routes in towns. The government railway is currently out of service, although there are plans afoot to divest it to private sector companies.

All licensed taxicabs carry red Public Passenger Vehicle (PPV) license plates. You can safely ignore the scale of fares printed on the doors. They have not been applicable for years. Some cabs are metered but the meters don't work. Fares tend to fluctuate (usually upwards) with the fluctuation in the exchange rate.

Efficient air-conditioned coaches and limousines link the major resort areas, or you can rent a vehicle, anything from a limousine with driver, to a self-drive car or a jeep, or even a moped. Renting a vehicle has the advantage of allowing you to set your own pace and schedule. Your own valid driver's license will suffice, or a valid international driver's license. But you will have to encounter some crazy driving and unfathomable traffic systems.

Public transportation

Breakdowns or Accidents

Major car rental firms have a 24-hour emergency service to handle anything from a breakdown to accidentally locking the keys in the car. If it is not stipulated or you are not sure, enquire from them what their recommended procedure is. Should you breakdown in the middle of nowhere with not a soul in sight, you'll find that people will magically materialize to volunteer assistance, most of whom consider themselves 'expert mechanics;' in truth, they will probably be able to get the vehicle going so that you can reach a phone for qualified assistance.

In these situations you should be sure to enquire what they propose to charge before they start tinkering. Occasionally, they will cheerfully wave the offer of money aside with the ubiquitous 'No problem;' more often they will request that you give them 'a money' or 'a smalls' (same thing, and it means a tip at your discretion). Do not flash a roll of US dollars at this juncture or the price will immediately become fixed and exorbitant. Depending on the problem and the degree of effort involved, anywhere between J$10–$50 should suffice.

Accidents should be reported to your car rental agency immediately. In case of injury, all major hotels have a doctor on call or can take the patient to the casualty department of the nearest hospital (*see list on page 83*).

Driving Tips

Driving in Jamaica, particularly in the major towns, is a real test of anyone's mettle. It doesn't help to get up-tight; it does help to remember that we drive on the left here. Also, you should be aware of the following points: we use our horns far more frequently than you are probably accustomed to, partly because you are as likely to encounter a cow, goat or dog, as you are to meet people wandering across the street. Stray dogs are killed on the roads with quite alarming frequency. We also like to greet people we know with a toot on the horn, or to say 'thank you' for courtesies from other drivers. We seldom indicate for turning or overtaking, and most of our hand signals defy interpretation. We seldom give advance warning of our presence on winding roads, we are impatient drivers and we are speed freaks, so it would be a good idea to advertize your presence. If you've ever driven in Rome, you'll be right at home here!

Jamaica is in the process of changing speed limit/distance signs to metric measurements. Until this is completed you will encounter a mixture of signs. Just remember that the speed limit in towns is 30mph or 50km; on the open road it is 50mph or 80km.

Only walk in the town centers

On Foot

Most Jamaican roads, with few exceptions and particularly outside of Kingston, were not designed with the pedestrian in mind. Sidewalks or pavements are often inadequate or missing entirely. Unless specifically mentioned, the itineraries in this book are meant to be driven.

By Air

The intra-island airline, Air Jamaica Express, has very good, regularly scheduled daily flights between Kingston, Montego Bay, Negril, Ocho Rios (Boscobel aerodrome 20 minutes from Ocho Rios) and Port Antonio. Best of all, they have an accident-free record. In Kingston tel: 923 8680/6664/9698 or 923 9498; Montego Bay: 952 5401/3; Negril: 957 4251; Ocho Rios: 975 3254; Port Antonio: 993 2405.

Air Jamaica Express and Airpack International (tel: 923 8557/0341/4290 and 6614) offer charter services, as do Helitours (Jamaica) Ltd. (tel: 974 2265 and 1108).

tions when planning your trip. Some questions which are useful in making decisions include: location – on the beach, hillside, in town, near amenities? Distance from airport, banks, shopping, restaurants? What does the price include – taxes and service charges?

The all-inclusive concept predominates at the larger hotels. In such places the price generally includes all meals and drinks, transportation to and from the airport, all sports and entertainment facilities, services and charges.

If you would rather not vacation with a crowd, there are private villas in a wide price range and most come with full- or part-time staff. Double check on transportation and enquire if there is a 24-hour emergency number.

The following list is by no means exhaustive but offers suggestions ranging from the expensive or luxury (not necessarily the same thing) end of the market, to the inexpensive or downright cheap.

As a guide to price categories, the following rates are for single occupancy, per room, EP (no meals included):
$$$ = US$135 to US$600; $$ = US$70 to US$130; $ = US$60 and under.

USEFUL INFORMATION

Baby-sitting

Two all-inclusive hotels currently cater for families with young children: the Franklin D Resort (FDR) in Runaway Bay (tel: 973 4591), and Boscobel Beach Hotel in St Mary (tel: 975 7330/6 and 975 3291). Nannies are available at both properties. Other hotels accept children but you may have to make your own arrangements for baby-sitting. If you are staying at a villa or guest house and a nanny is not part of the service offered, it is possible to arrange with the housekeeping staff to have someone baby-sit at reasonable rates. Jamaicans, as a rule, love children and are very good with them.

Maps

Road maps are available from any Jamaica Tourist Board office or Visitor Information Center. Alternatively, they are on sale in the major bookstores or from gas stations in or near the major resort towns.

HOURS & HOLIDAYS

Most business offices operate from 8.30am–4.30pm Monday to Friday. A few are open on Saturday. Banks open Monday to Thursday, 9am–2pm, Friday 9am–noon and 2.30pm–5pm, with few exceptions. Public holidays are: **New Year's Day** (January 1), **Ash Wednesday**, **Good Friday**, **Easter Monday**, **Labor Day** (May 23), **National Heroes' Day** (3rd Monday in October), **Christmas Day** (December 25) and **Boxing Day** (December 26).

ACCOMMODATION

The options are so numerous that final choice comes down to a matter of personal preference and budget. You can find what you want if you ask the right ques-

Kingston

JAMAICA PEGASUS HOTEL
Knutsford Boulevard
Tel: 926 3690/9
350 rooms, all amenities, popular with the business crowd. Very central. **$$$**

WYNDHAM NEW KINGSTON
Knutsford Boulevard
Tel: 926 5430/9
300 rooms with similar amenities/location to the Pegasus. Also popular with the business crowd. **$$$**

An important facility at any hotel

THE NEW COURTLEIGH HOTEL
85 Knutsford Blvd
Tel: 968 6339/40
110 rooms on one of the main roads in New Kingston. Easy access to the business district. Facilities for the disabled. Home to Mingles nightclub. **$$**

HOTEL FOUR SEASONS
18 Ruthven Road
Tel: 929 7655/7
79 rooms, slightly off the beaten track but still close to the action. Free transportation to nearby shopping plazas. **$$**

TERRA NOVA HOTEL
17 Waterloo Road
Tel: 926 9334/9
35 rooms, within walking distance of Devon House and a short taxi ride to shopping, restaurants, and nightlife. Offers free transportation to shopping plazas. **$$$**

MORGAN'S HARBOUR
Port Royal Road
Tel: 924 8464/5
45 rooms. Harbor-front hotel with marina. Offers several water-sports activities, also horse-back riding at stables nearby. Away from the bustle of Kingston, but still close enough to get to the central areas in about 30–45 minutes. **$$$**

MAYFAIR HOTEL
4 West Kings House Close
Tel: 926 1610
32 rooms, some in the main building, others in surrounding cottages. Charmingly informal in a quiet cul-de-sac. Great for families; extra beds or cot in rooms if required. **$**

SUTTON PLACE HOTEL
11 Ruthven Road
Tel: 926 2297
67 rooms, reasonable rates, easy access to central New Kingston. Disabled facilities. **$**

PINE GROVE GUEST HOUSE
near Content Gap in the
Blue Mountain range
Tel: 922 8705
Singles, suites, or chalet-style accommodation. A rustic retreat high above Kingston, yet only 30 minutes from Papine.

A high standard of service

You'll need your own transportation. Good walking trails. Cooking facilities in rooms but the restaurant offers good Jamaican cuisine. **$**

STRAWBERRY HILL HOTEL
Irish Town
Tel: 944 8400/7
18 suites and villas in this small luxury hotel and restaurant in the Blue Mountains, just outside Kingston. **$$$**

IVOR GUEST HOUSE
Jack's Hill
Tel: 977 0033
Continental breakfast is included. Very small (3 rooms), family-run guest house with the accent on personal service. Ideal retreat, romantic, great views. **$**

Montego Bay

HALF MOON GOLF & BEACH CLUB
Tel: 953 2211
421 rooms. Very luxurious, very beautiful. All amenities including one of the best golf courses on the north coast. Twenty minutes out of the town, free transportation to shops. Own beach, tennis courts, stables. **$$$**

ROUND HILL HOTEL & VILLAS
Tel: 952 5150/5
Smaller than the Half Moon, 110 rooms/villa suites; very luxurious and the most exclusive of the top-of-the-line hotels. Thirty minutes out of town on the road to Negril, with free transportation into town. All amenities – and then some. **$$$**

TRYALL GOLF & BEACH RESORT
Tel: 956 5660/3
With 52 rooms, the smallest of the top three Montego Bay luxury hotels, but the landscape and vistas are breathtaking. Home of the Johnnie Walker Championship Golf tournament. Superb golf course, good beach, all amenities. **$$$**

Sandals

SANDALS ROYAL CARIBBEAN
All-inclusive chain with hotels at Negril (1), Montego Bay (2) and Ocho Rios (2). Contact in Miami; tel: (305) 284 1300, fax: (305) 284 1336. In London; tel: 0171 581 9895, fax: 0171 823 8758. **$$$**

WYNDHAM ROSEHALL RESORT
Tel: 953 2650/9
About 20 minutes out of Montego Bay. Large (489 rooms), American-style hotel. They offer supervized children's program and free transportation to town. **$$$**

RICHMOND HILL INN
Top of Union Street
Tel: 952 3859
23 rooms with old world charm. Their rates include all meals (MAP), and they offer free transportation into town. **$$**

THE WEXFORD COURT HOTEL
39 Gloucester Avenue
Tel: 952 2854/5
61 rooms, centrally located; offers a range of water-sports, golf and tennis. **$$**

DOCTOR'S CAVE BEACH HOTEL
Opposite Doctor's Cave Beach
Gloucester Avenue
Tel: 952 4355/9
90 rooms, some suites, some apartments with cooking facilities. Very central. **$$**

FISHERMAN'S INN DIVE RESORT
Rock, near Falmouth
Tel: 954 3427
12 rooms. Not really Montego Bay, but only 30 minutes away. Ideal for water-sports. Quiet family resort. **$$**

CARIBLUE BEACH RESORT
Ironshore
Tel: 953 2250
Small, 20 rooms. Offers water sports activities and free transportation to town. **$**

PLANTATION INN
Main A4 road east of town
Tel: 974 5601/4
80 rooms of old world charm and traditional service. One of the few luxury hotels whose quoted rates include all meals. **$$$**

JAMAICA INN
Main A4 road east of town
Tel: 974 2514/8
45 rooms. This is another in the old world charm and service category, luxurious inn with good facilities. Rates also include all meals. **$$$**

Sans Souci

SANS SOUCI LIDO
Main A4 road east of town
Tel: 974 2353/5
111 rooms and suites; luxury spa, gym facilities. A SuperClub resort. The place to pamper yourself. Accepts children, but treat yourself if you can and go without them. **$$$**

JAMAICA GRANDE
On the beach off Main Street
Tel: 974 2201/9
Large (720 rooms) very American-style hotel, with artificial waterfall and lots of activity. **$$$**

COMMUNICATIONS AND NEWS

Kingston has two daily newspapers: *The Daily Gleaner* and *The Jamaica Observer*, and an evening tabloid, *The Star*, published by The Gleaner Company. These are distributed island-wide. Montego Bay's *Western Mirror* is a bi-weekly (Wednesday and Saturday) and there are several community newspapers island-wide. Publications for

80

A local post office – in touch with the world

visitors include the *Tourist Guide*, *The Visitor*, *Vacation Guide*, and *Destination Jamaica* which are put out by the Jamaica Hotel & Tourist Association (JHTA).

There are two television stations, JBC-TV and CVM, and 10 radio stations: RJR and its FM station FAME, JBC Radio 1 and 2, KLAS, IRIE-FM, LOVE-FM, POWER 106, HOT 102 and RADIO WAVES.

Every town has a post office and there are postal agencies in smaller districts. Your hotel will handle your mail for you if you wish or will be able to give you the current postal rates.

Phone Service

From outside: The regional code for dialing anywhere in Jamaica or the Caribbean is 876, followed by the area code and the number.

Calls within Jamaica: For long-distance calls, dial 0 then the seven-digit number. For local calls, dial all seven numbers. **Public call boxes**: To use one of these you need a Jamaican phonecard – available at all outlets (shops, pharmacies, etc.) displaying the 'phonecards on sale' sign. Even if you don't see a sign, ask. Occasionally the sign is missing. Phonecards can presently be used to make **local calls only**, as there has been much abuse of the system for making direct-dialed overseas calls.

From Jamaica worldwide: Telecom-munications of Jamaica (TOJ) controls the telephone network and it is possible to reach almost anywhere in the world, 24 hours a day.

Collect calls: It is no longer possible to receive collect calls from overseas, again, due to abuse of the system, but it is still possible to make collect calls to the USA and Canada from a public call box, and you do not need a phonecard. For AT&T 'USA Direct': 0-800-872 2881; MCI 'CALL USA': 0-800-674 7000. Teleglobe – 'Canada Direct': 0-800-222 0016.

If you have a cellular phone, you may bring it with you, if you wish, but you will be charged a fee by customs at the airport. This fee is refundable on departure. Alternatively, TOJ offers cellular service to visitors, with a modest charge per minute for airtime. TOJ's offices around the island are open to the public Monday to Friday 8am–4pm. Head office: 51 Half Way Tree Road, Kingston, tel: 926 9700; Montego Bay, 25 Church Street, tel: 952 5550; Ocho Rios, tel: 974 1574/6; Mandeville, 24 Hargreaves Avenue, tel: 962 2231; Port Antonio, Allan Avenue, 993 2775. A full list of TOJ's offices is on page 5 of the telephone directory.

Another company called **Boatphone** (968 4000/1 or 997 4832), got its start by providing cellular service for charter vessels and private yachts. They now offer rentals to any visitor at prices which are quite competitive with hotel charges.

Jamaica is also linked to the rest of the world by facsimile and cable services, also available through TOJ or your hotel.

ATTRACTIONS

The following attractions do not fit into any of the itineraries but are definitely worth a visit. Your hotel tour desk or the Jamaica Tourist Board can give information on how to get to them. The tour desk should be able to book you on an outing if you prefer.

South Coast – St Elizabeth

Black River Swamp Safari – run by Charles Swaby and Sheila Chung, is an excellent one-hour excursion in a covered motor launch up the lower course of the Black River, Jamaica's longest navigable river (44 miles). Part of the river flows through a protected nature reserve, the Great Morass, a huge freshwater swamp and the largest remaining crocodile refuge in Jamaica. Many species of birds nest along the banks and there is good fishing about a mile from the river mouth.

Boats or canoes can be rented for private fishing expeditions.

Don't miss the YS Falls

YS Falls – on the Holland Estate, about half an hour out of Black River. A trip to these incredibly beautiful falls can be combined with the Black River Swamp Safari, with a break for lunch, at an all-inclusive price. Or you can just drive to the Falls on your own. Holland is a privately owned estate and the trip to the falls (from the parking lot) is by tractor-drawn jitney. Very scenic and you should definitely have your camera with you. Good fun swinging from the lianas to drop into the swimming pools. Life-guards are stationed at all the swimming spots. There are picnic grounds and a fantastic tree house in a massive tree at the entrance. A good place to take the children.

Montego Bay Environs

Appleton Estate Tour – This tour used to be done by train from Montego Bay, but with the decline of the railway, it is offered by bus, departing Montego Bay, traveling inland and across the mountains to the south coast. You can opt for the tour which goes directly to the estate, or take the longer route which includes stops at Middle Quarters, St Elizabeth, by the pepper shrimp vendors, a one-way trip on the Black River and a visit to the YS Falls. Video tour from the Hospitality Lounge of Appleton Estate, plus a walking tour of the distillery where the rum of the same name is made. Lunch is offered in the Hospitality Lounge as part of the tour, and there is a gift shop where you can make your purchases.

Hilton High Day Tour – 20 miles inland by air-conditioned coach to St Leonard's, Westmoreland. A walking tour of the plantation, plus side trips to Seaford Town, a German settlement from the 18th century. The blond-haired, blue-eyed descendants of these first Germans still live here. A full day tour with Jamaican breakfast and roast suckling pig lunch, with the return trip taking you through the unique formations of the Cockpit country, home of the western Maroons.

Spanish Town

Walking Tour of Spanish Town – only 20 minutes from Kingston, this 1½-hour tour of the old Spanish capital of the island, (founded in 1534) covers the historic remains from the 16th to the 19th century. Included are stops at an old-fashioned tailor's shop where some of the oldest Singer sewing machines still in existence continue to be used; a visit to a Jamaican home for a chat with the owner and a cool drink; also a tour of the first Anglican Cathedral to be built (circa1523), outside of

Cannon at Spanish Town

Nuttall Memorial
6 Caledonia Avenue, tel: 926 2139
Emergency: 929 1604

St Joseph's
22 Deanery Road, tel: 928 4955, 928 1080, 928 1083

University Hospital of the West Indies (UHWI), Mona, tel: 927 1620

The Tony Thwaites Wing of UHWI (for private patients), tel: 927 6520 or 6555, 927 9419 or 9874

The main hospital for Montego Bay and environs is:

The Cornwall Regional
Mount Salem, tel: 952 6683

Ambulance Service

The Medical Associates Ambulance, tel: 929 5531

Deluxe Ambulance Service Co (24 hour emergency service) 54 Molynes Road, Kingston, tel: 923 7415

Wings (Ja) Ltd, Air Ambulance, local & overseas, 24 hour service, tel: 923 5416

Credit Cards Lost or Stolen

American Express: 0-800-327 1267 to report loss and request a replacement.

Local reps: **Kingston**
9 Cecilio Avenue, tel: 929 3077; 926 4291

Montego Bay
32 Market Street, tel: 929 2586

Visa: Call AT&T operator, 0-800-8722 881 and place collect call to: 415-574 7700

MasterCard: Call AT&T operator, 0-800-8722 881 and place collect call to: 314-275 6690

Embassies, Consulates and High Commissions

All have their offices in Kingston.
Australian High Commission: 64 Knutsford Boulevard, tel: 926 3550/2; 926 3969

England. Since 1843 it has been the cathedral of the Jamaica diocese of the Church of England. Other features include well-preserved Georgian architecture and one of the oldest iron bridges in the Western Hemisphere.

USEFUL ADDRESSES

Emergency Numbers

Air/Sea Rescue 119
Police 119
Ambulance 110
Fire 110

Hospitals

These hospitals are all in Kingston.

Andrews Memorial
27 Hope Road
Daytime: 926 7401/2, 929 3821 or 5903, 9pm–8am: 926 7403

Bustamante Hospital for Children
Arthur Wint Drive, tel: 926 5721/5, 968 0300–9.

Kingston Public
North Street, tel: 922 0229, 922 0210, 922 0530/1

National Chest
Liguanea, tel: 927 7121 or 6421

Medical Associates
18 Tangerine Place, tel: 926 1401, 968 3505/6, 968 3533/5

Stay cool and don't bother your consul!

Jamaica

Head Office: 2 St Lucia Avenue, Kingston 5, tel: 929 9200/19

Montego Bay: Cornwall Beach, tel: 952 4425

Ocho Rios: Shop #7, Ocean Village Shopping Center, tel: 974 2570 or 2582/3

Black River: Hendriks Building, 2 High Street, tel: 965 2074

Port Antonio: City Center Plaza, tel: 993 2117

Negril: Shop No 9, Adrila Plaza, tel: 957 4489

United States

New York: 801 Second Avenue, 20th Floor, NY, tel: (212) 856 9727

Miami/Latin America: 1320 South Dixie Highway, Suite 1100, Coral Gables, FL, tel: (305) 665 0557

Philadelphia: 1315 Walnut Street, Suite 1505, Philadelphia, PA, tel: (215) 545 1061

Boston: 21 Merchants Row, 5th Floor, Boston, MA, tel: (617) 248 5811/12

Dallas: 8214 Westchester, Suite 500, Dallas, TX, tel: (214) 361 8778

Chicago: 36 South Wabash Avenue, Suite 1210, Chicago, IL, tel: (312) 346 1546,

Detroit: 26400 Lahser Road, Suite 114A, Southfield, MI, tel: (313) 948 9557

Los Angeles: 3440 Wilshire Boulevard, Suite 1207, Los Angeles, CA, tel: (213) 384 1123

Atlanta: 300 West Wieuca Road, NE, Suite 100-A, Atlanta, GA, tel: (404) 250 9971/2.

Canada

1 Eglington Avenue East, Suite 616, Toronto, Ontario, tel: (416) 482 7850

Europe

United Kingdom: 1–2 Prince Consort Road, London SW7 2BZ, tel: 0171-224 0505

France: c/o Target International, 32 rue de Ponthieu, 75008 Paris, tel: 1-45 63 42 01

Spain: Carrer Sergat, Espana SL, Apdo-Correos 30266, 08080, Barcelona, tel: 3-280 58 38

Austrian Consulate: 2 Ardenne Road, tel: 929 5259

British High Commission: 26 Trafalgar Road, tel: 926 9050/4, 926 1020/3

Canadian High Commission: 30 Knutsford Boulevard, tel: 926 1500, 926 1701

Chinese Embassy: 8 Seaview Avenue, tel: 927 0850, 927 6816

Cuban Embassy: 9 Trafalgar Road, tel: 978 0931/3

Danish Consulate General: 449 Spanish Town Road, tel: 923 5051

French Embassy: 13 Hillcrest Avenue, tel: 927 9811/2, 927 6466

German Embassy: 10 Waterloo Road, tel: 926 6728, 926 5665 or 6729

Indian High Commission: 4 Retreat Avenue, tel: 927 3114 or 927 4270

Italian Embassy: 10 Rovan Drive, tel: 978 1273–5

Japanese Embassy: 32 Trafalgar Road, tel: 929 7534, 929 3338/9

Mexican Embassy: 36 Trafalgar Road, tel: 926 6891, 926 4242

Spanish Embassy: 25 Dominica Drive, tel: 929 6710, 929 8575

Swedish Consulate: 20 Bell Road, tel: 923 7114

Trinidad & Tobago High Commission: 60 Knutsford Boulevard, tel: 926 5730, 926 5739

United States Embassy: 2 Oxford Road, tel: 926 5679, 929 4850

Italy: c/o Sergat Italia SRI, Via Monte de Cenci 20, 00186 Rome, tel: 6-686 91 12

Germany: Postfach 900437, 60444 Frankfurt, tel: 61-8499 0044

Far East

Japan: #3 Mori Building, 1-4-10 Nishi Shinbashi, Minato-Ku, Tokyo 105, tel: 03-3591 3841

FURTHER READING

Insight Guide: Jamaica, Apa Publications, Hong Kong, edited by Paul Zach. A comprehensive survey of this island nation, with detailed essays on key topical subjects, and chapters profiling its main attractions, from reggae to cricket, as well as an insight into Jamaica's hidden corners.

Adams, C Dennis, *Flowering Plants of Jamaica*. Mona: University of the West Indies.

Barrett, Leonard E, *The Rastafarians: The Dread-locks of Jamaica*. London: Heinemann.

Beckwith, Martha, *Jamaican Proverbs*. New York: Negro University Press.

Black, Clinton V, *History of Jamaica*. London: Collins.

The Story of Jamaica. London: Collins.

Tales of Old Jamaica. Kingston: Sangster.

Boot, Adrian, *Jamaica: Babylon on a Thin Wire*. London: Thames & Hudson.

Brown, Aggrey, *Color, Class & Politics in Jamaica*. New Jersey: Transaction Books.

Chen, Ray, *Jamaica: The Beauty & The Soul of The Land We Love*. Kingston: Periwinkle Publishers.

Green, Jonathan, *Bob Marley & The Wailers*. London: Wise Publications.

Hart, Richard, *The Origins & Development of the People of Jamaica*. Montreal: International Caribbean Service Bureau.

Robinson, Carey, *The Fighting Maroons of Jamaica*. London: Collins/Sangster.

Fight for Freedom. Kingston: Kingston Publishers Ltd.

Senior, Olive, *A to Z of Jamaican Heritage*.

Sherlock, Philip and Preston, Barbara, *Jamaica: The Fairest Isle*. London: Macmillan Press.

Sibley, Inez Knibb, *Dictionary of Place-Names in Jamaica*. Kingston: Institute of Jamaica.

Wright, Philip, *Lady Nugent's Journal: of her residence in Jamaica from 1801 to 1805*. Kingston: Institute of Jamaica, 1966.

Wright, Richardson, *Revels in Jamaica 1682–1838*. New York: Dodd, Mead.

A perfect end to the day

Index

ACKNOWLEDGMENTS

Photography Rey Chen *and*
29B Anthony DaCosta
8–9, 23, 24B, 42T & B, 43, 44T, Hans Höfer
53, 58, 61T, 64, 66T, 74T, 81, 83, 85
16, 52, 26, 27, 52T, 60, 61B, Jamaica Tourist Board
65, 76, 80T
11, 12, 13, 14, 15, 41T, 54, 71 National Library, Jamaica
5B, 2–3, 28, 30B, 41B, 49, 50, 55, Carl Purcell
57T, 59, 66B, 75, 78B, 79, 80B, 84
Handwriting V.Barl
Cover Design Klaus Geisler
Cartography Berndtson & Berndtson